Celebrations

Celebrations

Original ideas for celebrating the seasons

SHARON AMOS

COLLINS & BROWN

First published in Great Britain in 2000
by Collins & Brown Limited
London House
Great Eastern Wharf
Parkgate Road
London SW11 4NQ

Distributed in the United States and Canada by Sterling Publishing Co.,
387 Park Avenue South,
New York,
NY10016, USA

1 3 5 7 9 8 6 4 2

British Library Cataloguing-in-Publication Data:
A catalogue record for this book is available from the British Library.

ISBN 1 85585 750 2

Conceived, edited and designed by Collins & Brown Limited

Editorial Director: Kate Kirby
Project Editor: Gillian Haslam
Copy Editor: Alison Wormleighton
Designer: Christine Wood

Reproduction by Classic Scan, Singapore
Printed and bound in Singapore

$\mathcal{C}$ONTENTS

FOREWORD

by Susy Smith
Editor, Country Living magazine

Throughout the year there are key dates in the calendar that unite families and bring friends together to celebrate. Some are ancient feasts and festivals, while others are simply special ways of enjoying each other's company at different times of the year.

Many of the occasions have close links to the seasons and reflect our agricultural past, when planting and harvesting dictated holidays and high days. All help us to understand our heritage. Throughout the year *Country Living* magazine celebrates these special occasions in its own inimitable style with inspiring photographs and thoughtful prose. This book is a collection of those pictures and words which together create a unique insight into the timeless and traditional customs we all love to celebrate.

Susy Smith

Introduction

Celebrations unveils the origins of the classic events we celebrate throughout the year and is full of practical suggestions, both new and traditional, for ways of enjoying them with family and friends. Some celebrations require weeks of planning, while others need no more preparation than a packet of sandwiches, a Thermos flask of tea and a picnic rug.

Spring brings Valentine's Day, Easter and the first flowers of the year to cheer the passing of winter. In summer thoughts turn to outdoor picnics, days at the beach, and garden parties. Autumn means harvest in the country calendar, Halloween and the time for woodland walks; and the year draws to a close with preparations for Christmas and New Year celebrations. Each seasonal chapter ends with a special 'Practicalities' section providing instructions for creating many of the ideas shown in the book, from flower arrangements to traditional recipes and simple makes.

From a springtime snowdrop walk to a Christmas carol concert, from a summer wedding to a harvest supper, with this book you won't be short of ideas for celebrating life all year round.

Spring

SPRING FLOWERS

One of the earliest signs of spring is the welcome appearance of the snowdrop. 'Chaste snowdrop, venturous harbinger of spring,' wrote Wordsworth. Yet rejoicing at spring's arrival with the very first flowers can be a little hasty. Snowdrops begin to flower when the weather is still decidedly wintry – their leaf tips are tough enough to push up through frozen ground. Not for nothing are they called *perce-neige* in France and snow piercers in parts of Britain.

The time to celebrate spring with a snowdrop walk is when sheets of snowdrops are in full flower. Many country estates and gardens open in early spring especially for such events. If there isn't a

snowdrop walk or day taking place in your area, it is well worth strolling around local churchyards, as snowdrops and churches have a special affinity. Many churchyards were planted with snowdrops so that plenty of flowers would be available to decorate the church for Candlemas on February 2nd, to celebrate the feast of the Purification of the Virgin Mary. Until the early 20th century, in some village churches Christmas greenery was not taken down until Candlemas, when jugs and bowls of snowdrops were carried in to take its place.

Wherever you go to appreciate snowdrops in spring, it's best not to plan to come away with a posy. Not only is the practice frowned upon from a conservation point of view, but many people still consider snowdrops unlucky flowers to be brought into the house – perhaps because of a Victorian belief that the flower structure resembled a corpse wrapped in a shroud. Enjoy them, instead, at their best, in vast numbers in a country churchyard or in a corner of your own garden.

BELOW LEFT: Other charming names for snowdrops include February fairmaids, Candlemas bells, Mary's taper and, more prosaically, snow piercer and dingle dangle.

BELOW CENTRE: Legend says that snowdrops were created by an angel to comfort Adam and Eve during a snowstorm. The snowflakes were transformed into flowers to reassure them that spring would return.

BELOW: On a snowdrop walk there will be precious few other flowers; perhaps a few early violets or grape hyacinths and some catkins or lambs' tails (shown here) – the male flowers of the hazel – in the hedgerow.

SPRING BULBS INDOORS

One way to steal a march on the garden and celebrate spring early is to encourage bulbs to flower ahead of season by growing them indoors. There's nothing quite like a bowl of scented narcissi or a fat waxy-petalled hyacinth to lift the spirits on a wintry day – their form and fragrance are a sensuous reminder that spring really is just around the corner.

The well-known Victorian gardening writer Mrs Theresa Earle described a popular way of displaying spring blooms, where a whole table or 'altarpiece' was dedicated solely to flowers: 'I am now staying with a friend… and her flower-table, standing in the window, looks charming… At the back are two tall glass vases with Pampas grass in them… a small Eucalyptus tree in a pot… a fine pot of Arums, just coming into flower; a small fern in front, and a bunch of paper-white Narcissus.'

There's no need to confine planting to conventional pots. The Victorians, for example, grew narcissi in pebbles and water, and hyacinths in special glass jars. Hyacinth jars are still available today, and ceramic mugs, cups or bowls also make ideal improvised pots for planting with bulbs. Use a layer of crumbled polystyrene for drainage, and fill them with a specially formulated bulb fibre or compost. Bulbs should be planted so that their tips are just showing, then left in a cool dark cupboard until growth begins. Whatever container you use, a few hours' preparation in autumn will ensure that you have a celebratory display of spring bulbs some weeks ahead of the garden.

LEFT: MATCH BULBS TO THE CONTAINER. HERE, SILVERY GALVANIZED POTS SET OFF PINK HYACINTHS TO PERFECTION. A HANDFUL OF MOSS PROVIDES THE FINISHING TOUCH AND COVERS UP ANY UNTIDY COMPOST. DON'T MIX DIFFERENT-COLOURED HYACINTHS IN ONE POT – THEY WON'T FLOWER AT THE SAME TIME.

BELOW: AN ANTIQUE SPONGEWARE MUG COMPLEMENTS A HYACINTH IN BOTH SCALE AND – EVENTUALLY – COLOUR.

BELOW RIGHT: A MIXED POSY OF GRAPE HYACINTHS AND SWEETLY SCENTED NARCISSI. THESE ARE AMONG THE MOST WELCOME OF EARLY SPRING FLOWERS AND ARE EASILY GROWN INDOORS.

BLUEBELL WOODS

The unforgettable sight of bluebells in bloom has been celebrated and commemorated by poets throughout the centuries. Inevitably, comparisons are drawn between the shimmering haze of the flowers and impressions of wood smoke or water between the trees. In his journal for 1871, priest and poet Gerard Manley Hopkins wrote: 'They come in falls of sky-colour washing the brows and slacks of the ground with vein-blue.'

The coming of the railway in the middle of the 19th century introduced a perfect way to appreciate a wood full of bluebells: from a slowly chugging steam train, without fear of stepping on and spoiling a single flower or leaf. It was nostalgia for these springtime journeys that helped save a small branch line threatened with closure in the 1950s – today the Bluebell Railway in Sussex is a major tourist attraction when the woods are thick with flowers. Similar sentiments were a spur for reviving bluebell celebrations across Britain, and today annual bluebell walks and bluebell teas help fund many local projects.

The vogue for wildflower gardening has led to some woods being stripped of their bulbs for resale, but insisting on proof of provenance before buying bluebell bulbs for the garden should help stamp out this practice. When picking bluebells from your garden, cut the stems rather than pulling them, to allow the bulb to build up strength for next year's flowering. The cut flowers are short-lived, but cutting them with only short stems helps them last longer.

RIGHT: THE REFLEXED PETALS OF THE BLUEBELL HAVE GIVEN RISE TO THE NAME *CRA'TAE* – CROW'S TOES – IN SCOTS DIALECT.

BELOW: ALTHOUGH BLUEBELLS ARE, BY NATURE, BLUE, THEIR COLOUR CAN VARY FROM LAVENDER TO INDIGO, AND BULBS WITH WHITE FLOWERS ARE NOT UNCOMMON.

BELOW RIGHT: BLUEBELLS BELONG TO THE LILY FAMILY. THEIR STICKY SAP, EVIDENT AS SOON AS THEY ARE PICKED, WAS USED IN MEDIEVAL TIMES AS A CRUDE PAPER GLUE.

VALENTINE'S DAY

Mid-February has been a time for celebrating love ever since the Roman festival of Lupercalia, which was held every year on February 15th. In honour of the goddess Juno, marriage and fertility, it was rather like a country fair. One of the customs was for young people to choose a sweetheart, or even just a good friend, for the year ahead. Over the centuries, this festival gradually merged with the feast-day of St Valentine – commemorating not one, but two third-century Roman martyrs, both called St Valentine. One was a priest in Rome who was clubbed to death for sheltering persecuted Christians; the other was a bishop who was martyred for holding forbidden weddings.

Legend has it that February 14th is also the day when birds choose their mates, hence the frequently used image of a pair of doves on Valentine's cards. In *A Midsummer Night's Dream*, Shakespeare wrote: 'Good morrow, friends. Saint Valentine is past;/Begin these wood-birds but to couple now?'

Love letters, handmade cards and poems have been exchanged by lovers on February 14th since the Middle Ages, but it was the Victorians who turned Valentine cards into high art. Some of the early cards were bawdy, to say the least, but towards the end of the 19th century, elaborate paper and cardboard confections embellished with lace and embroidery and sentimental verse appeared. These are treasured collectors' items today.

Red roses – which were believed to have been the flowers of Venus, the Roman goddess of love and beauty – became the traditional symbol of love in the Victorians' symbolic 'Language of Flowers'. Unfortunately, roses are completely out of season in the northern hemisphere in February, so lovers have had to rely on hothouse blooms or imported flowers.

The other unmistakable symbol of love is, of course, the heart. Heart-shaped trinket boxes are as popular now as they were in Victorian times. Likewise, earrings, brooches and other jewellery made in the form of hearts have always been favourite gifts for Valentine's Day.

RIGHT: A HEART-SHAPED WREATH MAKES A PERFECT VALENTINE'S GIFT. BUY A READYMADE WREATH FROM A FLORIST – THEY ARE USUALLY MADE OF PLIANT VINE STEMS – OR IF YOU HAVE THE CONFIDENCE, SHAPE ONE YOURSELF FROM FLEXIBLE GARDEN PRUNINGS. DECORATE THE WREATH WITH FRESH COUNTRY FLOWERS, FOR A FLEETINGLY BEAUTIFUL VALENTINE.

PREVIOUS PAGES: FLOWERS FOR THE TABLE AT EASTER INCLUDE HELLEBORES – THE PURPLE BLOOMS ARE SOMETIMES KNOWN AS LENTEN ROSES – PINK HYACINTHS, GREENISH-WHITE CLUSTERS OF GUELDER ROSES (*VIBURNUM OPULUS*) AND PARROT TULIPS, WHICH ARE PARTNERED HERE WITH PUNGENT CORIANDER LEAVES.

LEFT: AN EASTER TABLE SET FOR BREAKFAST WITH SPRING FLOWERS AND DECORATED HARD-BOILED HENS' EGGS, BOTH TRADITIONS THAT DATE BACK THOUSANDS OF YEARS.

RIGHT: HELLEBORES ARE IN FULL BLOOM AT EASTER AND THEIR SUBTLE SHADES ARE PERFECT FOR UNDERSTATED TABLE DECORATIONS.

FAR RIGHT: A POSY OF PRIMROSES DISPLAYED IN A DECORATED EGGSHELL HELD IN A DELICATE GLASS EGGCUP MAKES A PRETTY EASTER PLACE SETTING.

EASTER CELEBRATIONS

Our Easter celebrations are a glorious muddle of ancient pagan traditions and Christian customs. As Christianity spread, many of the pagan festivals were incorporated in the Christian celebrations. For example, great bonfires once blazed all over Europe to mark the return of the sun after a long cold winter. Today, fires are still lit on Easter Saturday – but they are dedicated to celebrating enlightenment spread by Christian teachings. The symbolism of fire is also used in church services. In Catholic churches on Easter Eve, all candles are extinguished, then the great Paschal candle is lit and from its flame all the other candles are rekindled. The custom of decorating churches with spring flowers and greenery at Easter bears more than a hint of the ancient Celtic practice of tree worship. Other Easter traditions, from decorating eggs to eating hot cross buns, have similarly pagan origins.

EASTER EGGS

At the original feast of Eostre, the goddess of spring, eggs were used to represent renewal and new life. Centuries later, Christians adopted the egg for their own purposes, using it as a potent symbol for the Resurrection. Ancient games like egg-rolling (originally performed to ensure good crops and large families) were reinterpreted for the Christian faith, so that the egg came to symbolize the rolling away of the stone from Christ's tomb. Egg-rolling is still popular in parts of England, Scotland, Switzerland and North America. One of the most spectacular versions of the game takes place on the lawns of the White House in Washington, DC, where crowds of children gather to roll more than 100,000 eggs.

French children still play catch with coloured hard-boiled eggs until someone drops one and the game is over. In Greece on Easter

BELOW LEFT: HENS' EGGS PAINTED IN A NATURALISTIC WAY TO COPY THE COLOURING OF DIFFERENT SPECIES OF BIRDS' EGGS ARE DISPLAYED IN A HUMBLE EGG BOX. THESE EGGS ARE PURELY DECORATIVE AS THEY HAVE BEEN COLOURED WITH PAINT RATHER THAN EDIBLE FOOD DYES.

Sunday, it's customary for people to carry a red egg with them; whenever two people meet, they tap their eggs together. One person says, 'Christ is risen', and the other responds, 'Truly he is risen'.

Decorating eggs is also an ancient practice. The custom of boiling eggs with onion skins to colour them golden-brown comes from Scandinavia and Switzerland – other natural dyes include spinach, beetroot, tea leaves and gorse blossom. Polishing the hard-boiled eggs with a little oil or butter brings out the colour, then they are ready to serve for breakfast on Easter Sunday. The decoration of hard-boiled eggs reached its height of popularity at the beginning of the 20th century. When bakers and confectioners began experimenting with sugar eggs and marzipan, and eventually the familiar chocolate eggs of today, the tradition of decorating hen's eggs declined.

BELOW: THE GENEROUS SIZE OF GOOSE EGGS MAKES THEM A LOT EASIER TO DECORATE. THE PATTERNS BELOW HAVE BEEN CREATED USING A WAX-RESIST TECHNIQUE. THE DESIGN IS PENCILLED LIGHTLY ONTO A HARD-BOILED EGG THEN DRAWN OVER WITH A WHITE WAX CRAYON. WHEN THICK PAINT IS APPLIED, THE WAXED AREAS RESIST THE COLOUR, LEAVING THE DESIGN WHITE.

EASTER BONNETS

Processions and parades are an integral part of Easter celebrations the world over and a perfect excuse to dress up. The item of clothing to receive the most special attention at Easter has always been the hat. When hats were worn every day, rather than reserved for weddings and gala events as tends to be the case today, it was only natural to jazz up an ordinary bonnet for special occasions. At Easter, real spring flowers, ribbons and artful paper flowers were all used to embellish normal headgear. In parades big and small, at national or village level, prizes were awarded to the best or most elaborate Easter bonnets. It's a custom that is still popular today with everyone from schoolchildren in classroom competitions to adults taking part in the vast Easter parades held all over the world. Parades are especially popular in Spain, particularly in Seville, where the Easter *feria*, or fair, lasts for days on end, and in Spanish-speaking Latin American countries such as Mexico.

LEFT: GETTING READY FOR AN EASTER PARADE. RABBITS HAVE A SPECIAL SIGNIFICANCE AT EASTER. THEY REPRESENT THE EASTER HARE, WHO WAS THE SACRED COMPANION OF EOSTRE, THE ANCIENT GODDESS OF SPRING. ALL OVER EUROPE, CHILDREN GET UP EARLY ON EASTER SUNDAY TO SEARCH FOR EGGS LEFT BY THE EASTER HARE OR RABBIT.

RIGHT: THESE EASTER BONNETS ARE MADE FROM COLOURED AND PAINTED CARD AND EMBELLISHED WITH PAPER STREAMERS, A FROTH OF LACY PAPER DOILIES AND SIMPLE FELT FLOWERS, IN TRUE PRIZE-WINNING STYLE.

EASTER FEASTS

Like other aspects of the festival, the custom of feasting at Easter predates Christianity. It was a natural way to rejoice at the passing of winter and lean times, and to celebrate the appearance of fresh food. Different foods have become an important part of Easter celebrations. Many European countries bake special Easter breads, some of which are decorated with eggs. There are Italian breads shaped like rabbits with hard-boiled eggs hidden in the stomachs, and plaited Greek loaves with dyed red eggs peeping between the strands. Traditional Russian Easter breads are tall and rounded and are topped with icing, like snow on the onion domes of their churches.

Instead of trying to outlaw the spicy buns originally baked in Britain in honour of the spring goddess, the Church wisely sanctified them by insisting on the addition of a dough cross and the condition that they were baked only on Good Friday. Although hot cross buns are baked in advance today, they are still eaten on Good Friday and are a flourishing tradition that has spread across the Atlantic.

Easter Day is a joyful feast-day after the solemnity of Good Friday. Roast lamb is traditionally served at lunchtime, a custom incorporated from the Jewish feast of the Passover. In Greece a whole lamb is spit-roasted, and in Italy lamb is often served with a salad of hard-boiled eggs; kid is the Easter speciality in Rome.

A traditional British Easter Sunday tea should always include a simnel cake. This rich fruit cake is topped with marzipan, brushed with egg white, and then lightly browned under the grill. Once the marzipan would have been in the form of small balls, representing the Apostles, but these days a simnel cake is just as likely to feature an Easter rabbit or hare.

FAR LEFT: A SIMNEL CAKE IS A BRITISH TRADITION AT EASTER. THIS ONE HAS A RABBIT MOULDED IN RELIEF ON THE MARZIPAN, A REFERENCE TO THE HARE WHO ACCOMPANIED EOSTRE, THE SPRING GODDESS. OVER THE YEARS, THE HARE HAS METAMORPHOSED INTO THE EASTER BUNNY.

LEFT: EVEN SHOP-BOUGHT BISCUITS CAN BE IMPROVED AND EMBELLISHED USING AN ICING BAG WITH A FINE NOZZLE. FOR AN EXTRA-SPECIAL EFFECT, LEAVE THEM TO SET, THEN TIE THE BISCUITS IN SMALL BUNDLES WITH NARROW RIBBON.

RIGHT: FOR HOMEMADE EASTER BISCUITS, USE A SHORTBREAD MIXTURE FOR THE BEST RESULTS, AND STAMP OUT THE BISCUITS WITH SHAPED DOUGH-CUTTERS. DON'T ICE THEM UNTIL THEY ARE COLD.

Pancakes are traditionally served on Shrove Tuesday, the day before Lent begins. Originally the aim was to use up butter and eggs, which were forbidden during Lent, and in fact Shrove Tuesday – or Mardi Gras ('fat Tuesday') – was a day of feasting and carnivals. For families today, part of the fun of 'Pancake Day' is cooking the pancakes. For extra-light pancake batter, try substituting beer or fizzy water for some of the milk.

Use a simple shortbread recipe for successful Easter biscuits. Sieve 150g (6oz) flour into a bowl and stir in 50g (2oz) castor sugar; knead in 100g (4oz) butter with your hands until the mixture binds together. Roll it out carefully until it is about 1cm (½in) thick, and stamp out shapes using biscuit cutters. Bake them on a baking sheet in a moderate oven until golden brown – about 20 minutes. Leave to cool before decorating.

Make a Valentine's wreath from dried rosebuds, which are sold by weight by stockists of dried flowers and pot-pourri. The easiest method is to thread the rosebuds directly onto florist's stub wire and then shape the wire into a heart. Tape the ends of the wire together at top centre, and cover with a frill of lace. For a scented wreath, add a few drops of rose or rose geranium oil.

Hyacinths can be forced into early flowering in hyacinth jars. Fill the jar with water almost up to the neck, then place the bulb in the top. Keep it in a cool, dark place for eight to ten weeks, until the flower bud is about 5cm (2in) tall, then move it into a warmer, lighter place. Top up the water level as necessary. Or instead of putting the jars in a dark cupboard, you could use the Scandinavian technique of covering the bulbs with paper cones – make them from newspaper or wallpaper as the fancy takes you.

All sorts of spring-flowering shrubs and trees can be encouraged into bloom by bringing the branches into a warm room and standing them in a vase of water. Try apple twigs, forsythia, pussy willow and flowering currant for a cheerful spring flower-table. A branch of winter-sweet (*Chimonanthus*) with its strange, tasselled flowers will perfume a whole room. Other favourites for forcing include daphne, witch hazel, wisteria, and flowering quince, cherry and plum. Choose heavily budded, substantial stems for the best results.

The technique of *Scherenschnitte*, or paper-cutting, which originated in Germany and Switzerland, can be used to decorate hens' eggs for Easter. Plain coloured paper looks best as it doesn't detract from the shape. Cut symmetrical designs on the fold for the central images and use pinking shears to cut strips for decorative borders. Glue the paper designs onto the egg with wallpaper paste and add a protective coat of varnish when the paste has dried.

Découpage is another way to adorn eggs. Cut out images from magazines or buy ready-printed sheets of designs as the Victorians did. Blowing the eggs first instead of boiling them will make them last longer (and they will also be light enough to be hung from a branch if you want to make an Easter egg 'tree'). Prick the top and bottom of each egg with a pin, break the yolk with a thin wire and then blow gently through one hole to force the contents out the other. Wash out the eggs carefully and leave to dry before decorating.

Amaryllis (*Hippeastrum*) are classic indoor spring-flowering bulbs. (They are natives of South America and are not hardy in the northern hemisphere.) Pot them up so that half the bulb sits above the surface of the compost, and then water sparingly until they begin to grow, when you can step up the watering and add a liquid feed every ten days or so. There's no need to start them off in the dark. To stimulate the same bulbs into growth the following year, cut off all the leaves and stand them next to a radiator.

Growing spring bulbs in pebbles was a popular Victorian technique. To copy the effect, buy pebbles from a garden centre. (It's illegal to take them from the seaside and in any case it would be difficult to get rid of their salty residue.) Fill a glass vase with the pebbles and set a hyacinth bulb on top, surrounded by a few extra supporting pebbles. Narcissi can be planted deeper. Now add water but don't let it touch the base of the bulb.

When cutting garden flowers it's important to put them *immediately* into water, rather than carting them around the garden in a basket as you seek out more flowers. A well-scrubbed can with a few centimetres (an inch or so) of water in the base makes a lightweight, unbreakable collecting tin. Choose a ring-pull style can so there won't be any sharp edges. You could also add a knotted string handle for carrying.

Create a miniature indoor spring garden. Line a wire basket with a layer of moss, then insert a fibrous hanging-basket liner filled with compost. Plant it up with a selection of spring bulbs such as grape hyacinths (*Muscari*), dwarf iris (*Iris reticulata*) and 'Tête-à-tête' narcissi. Keep the basket in the dark, then when the bulbs have come through, bring it into the light and add a primula or two. Once the bulbs and primulas have finished flowering, you can replant them in the garden for next spring.

Fill a pretty frame with appliquéd hearts for a permanent Valentine's keepsake. Cut a piece of cardboard to fit inside the frame and then cut a piece of plain linen a little larger than the cardboard. Appliqué fabric hearts to the linen, either using traditional hand stitching around the edges or using bonding web which is applied with an iron. Stretch the linen over the cardboard, and fold and stitch the corners to secure, then mount it in the frame.

Snowdrops make enchanting posies encircled with ivy leaves, which echo the green tips of their petals. Pick the stalks as long as possible and tie the posy with natural raffia, then give the posy as a token to herald spring's arrival. Country estates used to send boxes of such posies to market in spring, and one or two still do. But be prepared to encounter a lingering superstition in some parts of Britain that snowdrops shouldn't be brought indoors.

Turn a simple summer straw hat into a fetching Easter bonnet for the day by trimming the brim with a length of antique lace secured with a hatpin. Tuck sprays of apple blossom and tightly furled rosebuds into the band of lace. Or, for a bolder look, make a hat band of petersham (grosgrain) ribbon and add appropriate flowers – deep indigo ribbon, for example, would look good with a small bunch of purple anemones.

Make cheerful egg cosies from felt for Easter breakfast eggs. Cut two identical shapes – a crown or a cap, for example – and sew them together using blanket stitch or another simple hand stitch. Sew on small tassels or tiny beads for decoration. To make a ruff for the egg to sit on, take a circle of felt and cut a hole in the centre to fit snugly around the egg. Trim the edge into points. You could also paint faces or shapes on the eggs with a fine paintbrush, but use food colouring not paint for this, as the eggs will be eaten. At Easter some stationers sell egg-decorating kits that use edible colours.

For a special Valentine's Day tea, dust small cupcakes with icing sugar (confectioner's sugar) and decorate them with fondant hearts. Buy the fondant ready-made from the supermarket, knead some red food colouring into it, then roll out the fondant and use a heart-shaped cutter to stamp out the decorations. Stick the fondant shapes to the cakes either with sieved raspberry jam or with a dab of buttercream made from 25g (1oz) softened butter, 50g (2oz) icing sugar and a squeeze of lemon juice, mixed together with a fork until smooth.

Summer

MIDSUMMER'S DAY

The longest day of the year – Midsummer's Day – used to be celebrated all over Europe with huge bonfires that were lit to honour the sun and ensure a good harvest. Girls and boys would leap over the flames to encourage the crops to grow tall. In some regions, sweethearts would throw wreaths to each other across the fire – woe betide anyone who dropped one. Midsummer bonfires were also credited with protecting the village from witchcraft, and it was considered good luck to kindle the kitchen range with an ember from the fire. Now we prefer to mark the longest day a little more sedately – with, perhaps, lunch in the garden, a picnic or supper under the stars.

LEFT: EVEN IF YOU CARRY YOUR PICNIC ONLY AS FAR AS THE POTTING SHED, IT CAN STILL FEEL LIKE A SPECIAL OCCASION. HERE, NEW ORLEANS-STYLE *MUFFULETTA* – A ROUND LOAF CRAMMED TO BURSTING WITH PARMA HAM, BEEFSTEAK TOMATOES AND SALAD LEAVES – IS WASHED DOWN WITH A GLASS OF BEER.

RIGHT: YOU CAN PLAN A PICNIC DOWN TO THE LAST DETAIL, BUT THE WEATHER ALWAYS PLAYS THE WILD CARD.

BELOW: FOLDING CHAIRS AND STOOLS, PLUS
CUSHIONS AND RUGS, ALLOW YOU TO SET UP CAMP
FOR THE DAY WHEREVER YOU GO, SO THEY ARE AN
INDISPENSABLE PART OF YOUR KIT.

EASY LIVING

In a prolonged spell of hot weather, there's no better to way
to celebrate summer than by moving out of doors. All the
clichés about turning your garden into an outdoor room
start to make sense when you set up a permanent dining
table under the shade of an apple tree or vine arbour and
sling a hammock between two sturdy posts.

High summer is one of the few times gardeners don't
curse the shadow cast by a weeping willow or spreading
branches of a beech tree, but unless your garden is naturally
shady, you'll need to arrange some sort of protection from
the sun. A big garden parasol will shade the table at
lunchtime but a simple canopy is even more versatile and
relatively easy to make (see overleaf).

Furniture not only brings indoor comfort outside, but
also adds visual interest to a garden. It needs to be informal,
adaptable, reasonably comfortable and, if it is to be left
outside, weatherproof. Permanent dining furniture for the
garden is undoubtedly a convenience, as it allows
impromptu alfresco meals to be enjoyed on the spur of the
moment, and it can easily be supplemented with folding
chairs if necessary. Rugs and cushions for garden furniture
can be brought out of storage and positioned invitingly on
the grass and on seats (though it is best to put them under
cover at night, otherwise the dew would eventually cause
them to rot).

To make your garden 'room' look planned and purposeful,
rather than an afterthought or a jumble of cast-off chairs,
spend a few hours giving furniture a makeover. A coat of
gloss paint or coloured woodstain will bring unity to a
mismatched assortment of garden dining chairs. Folding
canvas director's chairs can be updated with new loose
covers that quickly slip in place. Or, for a less temporary
treatment, take the old fabric off completely and recover
chairs, nailing the new fabric in place with upholstery tacks.
Modern deckchairs often come with detachable 'slings' (the
fabric part), so that you can change their appearance at whim.
Older ones will need to be stripped and new canvas nailed
on. Once everything has been overhauled and set in place,
you'll have time to sit back in the sun and admire your
handiwork all summer long.

LEFT: THIS HAND-KNOTTED HAMMOCK HAS BEEN FITTED WITH A WOODEN SPREADER BAR TO HOLD THE NET OPEN, MAKING IT EASIER TO CLIMB INTO.

BELOW: STRING HAMMOCKS ARE OFTEN SOLD VIA MAIL ORDER CATALOGUES OR CLASSIFIED ADS, AS WELL AS IN GARDEN CENTRES OR HOME STORES. IF YOU'RE FAIRLY NIMBLE-FINGERED, YOU MIGHT WANT TO TRY YOUR HAND AT MAKING ONE YOURSELF. THE BASIC KNOT USED IS THE SHEET BEND. LOOK FOR A CRAFT BOOK IN YOUR LOCAL LIBRARY FOR FULL INSTRUCTIONS.

RIGHT: A PORTABLE SUN CANOPY IS IDEAL
FOR THE GARDEN AND FOR PICNICS TOO,
AND IT IS EASY TO MAKE. SEW TWO
LENGTHS OF STRONG CANVAS TOGETHER,
THEN HEM THE EDGES. ADD A LARGE
BRASS EYELET TO EACH CORNER, THROUGH
WHICH YOU CAN THREAD ROPE. THE
CORNERS OF THIS CANOPY ARE ROPED TO
TWO NEARBY TREES, WHILE HAZEL POLES
FORM THE REMAINING TWO SUPPORTS.
THE CANOPY IS SIMPLY TIED TO THE TREES
AND SUPPORTS, BUT THE HAZEL POLES
NEED SEPARATE GUY ROPES TO HOLD
THEM SAFELY UPRIGHT.

LEFT: Don't neglect pudding lovers on a picnic. Robust chocolate sponge bars with a chocolate-and-nut topping will travel unscathed in an old-fashioned sandwich tin.

BELOW: Flat Italian focaccia bread is made with olive oil. Anchovies, olives and grilled peppers are an appropriate Mediterranean filling.

BELOW: FOR VERY SPECIAL OCCASIONS, SPARE NO EFFORT AND PACK PROPER SILVERWARE, LINEN NAPKINS AND REAL CHINA TO EAT FROM. JUST MAKE SURE EVERYONE TAKES TURNS CARRYING THE HAMPER.

PICNIC FARE

What better way to mark the longest day of the year than with a picnic? It can be as simple or as extravagant as you like. At its most basic, a sandwich, a bar of chocolate and an apple will sustain you on a long hike; at its most elaborate, there will be hampers packed with real silverware and proper wine glasses, in addition to more ambitious dishes.

For spur of the moment celebrations, no-preparation foods like bags of ready-washed salad, tubs of hummus and taramasalata, plus easy-to-eat fruits like cherries, strawberries and grapes, are invaluable. For grander picnics, there are plenty of foods that can be prepared the day before and will actually benefit from being given time for the flavours to develop and blend.

For instance, *tartines* – Provençal-style sandwiches – are far removed from two thin slices of bread with a sliver of cheese. They are made by cutting a baguette in half lengthwise, rubbing the inside with a clove of garlic and then filling the loaf with a mixture of anchovies, olives, chopped pepper and tomatoes, mashed together with olive oil and lemon juice. Wrapping the finished *tartine* in foil or greaseproof paper, tying it together with string for good measure and weighting it down with a chopping board topped with something heavy – three or four cans of beans should do the trick – creates a delicious, moist sandwich.

A similar idea comes from New Orleans: instead of a baguette, the *muffuletta* (pictured on page 36) uses a round loaf, split in half and filled with an assortment of cheeses, salami, pickles and olives. To serve, it is cut in wedges like a cake.

Supermarkets also stock such a vast variety of breads from around the world that picnic sandwiches need never be boring. Pitta breads are perfect for fillings like a Greek salad of chopped tomato, cucumber, onion, olives and small cubes of feta cheese, while Italian focaccia goes well with a grilled-pepper salad or Parma ham and rocket.

Hefty omelettes packed with vegetables make perfect picnic food served in substantial wedges, rather like a quiche without the pastry. Potatoes feature heavily in a Spanish *tortilla* – waxy salad potatoes will give the best results. Cut them into tiny dice, and fry them for close to an hour before tipping in the beaten eggs; or slice the potatoes into rounds, blanch and then fry. An Italian *frittata* includes peppers and broad beans (fava beans), while in the Middle East, *eggah* is an omelette-style dish packed with aubergine (eggplant) or sometimes spinach, but baked in the oven rather than fried. All of these are easily portable dishes: pack them on plates, wrapped in foil, then cut and serve them at the picnic.

Fresh fruit is the easiest option to offer next, but you could cater for guests who expect a pudding by baking a batch of your favourite flapjacks or brownies to bring along. A classic loaf-shaped fruitcake, which is also easy to carry and slice, and not too messy to eat, makes a satisfying conclusion to the perfect picnic.

GARDEN PARTY

Anyone fortunate enough to have a summer birthday can celebrate with a garden party. The essential ingredients are good food, plenty to drink and, of course, good weather. (As a contingency it may be wise, for a large group, to hire a marquee or sweep out a barn ready for a quick retreat.) No matter how informal the setting, do guests the courtesy of scrubbing down garden furniture and checking for splinters.

Old trestle tables and garden furniture can be dressed up to suit the occasion. Having a decorating theme helps in this respect. For example, assorted tables can be linked by covering them in damask cloths, and repeating flowers and coloured glass for each setting. As dusk falls, add candles for a touch of romance. Instead of storm lanterns, improvise with nightlights (votives) in jam jars if a breeze gets up.

Give guests a hint of the special celebrations to come by making your own invitations and personalizing them with ribbons or old photographs. Follow the theme through by providing tiny mementoes for guests to take away, rather like wedding favours. Small, extravagantly wrapped parcels of sweets or miniature boxes of chocolates make perfect parting gifts to say thank you for coming.

RIGHT: AN INFORMAL CAKE, FINISHED WITH SOFT CREAMY ICING TEASED INTO PEAKS WITH A FORK, IS CRAMMED WITH CANDLES OF EVERY COLOUR.

FAR RIGHT: A GARDEN TABLE IS DRESSED WITH A DAMASK CLOTH AND SET WITH OLD BLUE-AND-WHITE CHINA, BLUE GLASS AND LINEN NAPKINS. FOR AN INFORMAL PARTY, MIXING AND MATCHING FAVOURITE PIECES LENDS CHARACTER TO THE SETTING.

GARDEN PARTY FOOD

A rather neglected meal in this day and age, afternoon tea rarely seems to fit into the working day, but a garden party is the one time when an extravagant tea is entirely appropriate. The ritual harks back to the 1930s, when tennis parties were all the rage and players needed sustenance between matches, and it has been popular ever since.

Entertaining with Elizabeth Craig, every successful hostess's etiquette and style bible of that era, has lots of tips and suggestions that today sound as enticing as ever. One of her ideas was to send out invitations inscribed with the magic words 'Strawberries & Tea'. For a country setting she recommended serving strawberries unhulled, piled in rustic baskets and accompanied by cream poured into miniature pails, and decorating the handles of both with strawberry leaves. Her menu for a more substantial tea, leading up to a strawberry feast, included 'tiny hot buttered scones, a plate of cucumber sandwiches, a plate of bridge rolls filled with chopped smoked salmon seasoned with freshly ground black pepper, a plate of brown sandwiches filled with chopped fried mushrooms, and a plate of thin toast, split, buttered and filled with flaked tunny fish moistened with mayonnaise and seasoned to taste with paprika'.

BELOW LEFT: A GATEAU DECORATED WITH CURLS OF SHAVED CHOCOLATE AND FRESH REDCURRANTS. IF YOU DON'T HAVE THE CONFIDENCE, OR TIME, TO BAKE A SPECTACULAR CAKE, CUSTOMIZE A SHOP-BOUGHT ONE WITH SIMILAR GARNISHES FOR HOMEMADE APPEAL.

BELOW: SUMMER PUDDINGS ARE DRIZZLED WITH A BLACKCURRANT SAUCE AND ORNAMENTED WITH SPRIGS OF SWEET CICELY. INDIVIDUAL SUMMER PUDDINGS ARE EASIER TO SERVE AND EAT THAN SEGMENTS CUT FROM A LARGE VERSION.

An accompanying cup of afternoon tea should be delicate and light: a China brew like broken orange pekoe or a refreshing Assam would be suitable. If you are serving chilled white or sparkling wine, a fan of sliced strawberries in each glass will look pretty and continue the theme. Children and non-drinkers won't feel forgotten if you make jugs of real lemonade for them. Start with a syrup made by gently poaching the peel of three lemons in a little water. Strain the cooled liquid into a bottle and add the juice of the lemons and plenty of sugar. Shake the bottle to dissolve the sugar, then pour generous servings into jugs and dilute with sparkling mineral water. Real orangeade can be made in exactly the same way, using three oranges plus a lemon for extra tang.

While strawberries are unsurpassed served on their own, other summer fruits can become spectacular puddings. A proper homemade jelly will be appreciated by children and adults alike: redcurrants and raspberries make perfect partners puréed together and coaxed into a softly setting jelly with cornflour (cornstarch).

Garnish puddings with the ultimate edible decoration: frosted redcurrants. Whisk an egg white in one bowl and fill another with castor sugar; dip clusters of perfect berries into the egg white, then into the sugar; shake gently and leave to dry on a sheet of baking parchment. Guests won't be able to resist them.

BELOW: SUMMER AFTERNOON TEA WOULD BE INCOMPLETE WITHOUT HOMEMADE SCONES, STRAWBERRY JAM AND THICK, THICK CREAM.

BELOW RIGHT: VASES OF SUMMER FLOWERS FROM THE GARDEN ECHO THE ROSE MOTIF ON AN ANTIQUE QUILT, USED AS A SOFT COVER ON THIS TABLE SET FOR AN INFORMAL AFTERNOON TEA.

BELOW: PAPER LANTERNS HUNG FROM THE CANOPY OF TREES ADD TO THE GENERAL AIR OF FESTIVITY, WHILE PITCH FLARES SAFELY CONTAINED IN IRON HOLDERS CAST A WARM AND INVITING GLOW OVER THE TABLE.

A MIDSUMMER'S EVE PARTY

To celebrate the longest day, it makes sense to hold an outdoor party. With any luck, the sky will remain light well into the evening, but you will still need supplementary lighting. Lighting becomes all-important at an evening gathering, which has different priorities to a daylight party. Apart from any other considerations, you don't want guests blundering into ponds or falling down steps. However, you don't need full-beam security lights or glaring floodlights: low-level electric or solar-powered lights, fitted with spikes to stick into the ground along a path or among plants, are effective without being overpowering. Electric fairy lights, candles and nightlights (votives), storm lanterns, hurricane lamps, flares or even gas-mantle lamps will also do the job.

You'll need to light a path to and from the house: fairy lights strung through a hedge look pretty, and nightlights, set in jam jars and placed at ground level, can be used to illuminate steps. (Use tapers to light the nightlights.) Another way of creating an atmospheric glow is to put sand in large, flat-bottomed brown-paper bags and then place a candle in the sand in each bag.

Candles can be used to shed light on the table, too, while hurricane lamps hung from trees or garden arches and arbours cast a wider glow; check them regularly and have plenty of spare candles to replace any that are burning low. Scented candles – especially those perfumed with oil of citronella – perform a dual role, as they also help to ward off biting insects like mosquitoes and midges.

The American author F Scott Fitzgerald knew how to throw a party with panache, and in Fitzgerald's 1925 novel *The Great Gatsby*, the eponymous hero spared no expense to ensure that everybody had a good time, as his neighbour relates: 'There was music from my neighbor's house through the summer nights. In his blue gardens men and girls came and went like moths among the whisperings and the champagne and the stars... At least once a fortnight a corps of caterers came down with several hundred feet of canvas and enough colored lights to make a Christmas tree of Gatsby's enormous garden. On buffet tables, garnished with glistening hors d'oeuvre, spiced baked hams crowded against salads of harlequin designs and pastry pigs and turkeys bewitched to a dark gold.'

Even if you don't go to quite the same lengths, you can still put time and effort into making sure things go smoothly. If the evening turns cool, a hot supper dish will warm everyone up. A barbecue is the easiest way to cook out of doors, but think up some alternatives to predictable sausages and burgers. Chicken wings marinated in and glazed with an orange sauce or spiced up with a chilli and tomato salsa; spare ribs coated in honey, soy sauce, ginger and garlic; vegetable kebabs with cubes of aubergine (eggplant), pepper, courgette (zucchini), mushrooms and slices of corn on the cob, brushed with olive oil and lemon juice and char-grilled over the coals – all of these add up to a memorable party.

DRESSING THE TABLE

A beautifully dressed table is a key part of any summer celebration. It reveals just how much care and thought have gone into making the party a success. Whether you're planning a garden party for 50 or an intimate candlelit supper, it's a good idea to have a theme in mind to decorate the table. The food may suggest a colour scheme: afternoon tea with strawberries and raspberries can be enhanced with jugs of pink, red and cream roses, old-fashioned pinks (Dianthus), pink stocks (*Matthiola*) and pink, red and white sweet peas.

Or let your favourite china be the starting point. Blue-and-white willow-pattern plates can be teamed with plain blue china bowls and glassware with a tint of blue. Blue summer flowers to decorate the table could include deep indigo delphiniums, pale blue love-in-a-mist, whose flowers are framed in a filigree of ferny green, and campanulas tall and small. To add a touch of blue to the food, float starry blue borage flowers in fruit drinks or scatter them across salads – they taste faintly of cucumber.

For sheer sophistication, set the table in silver and white: it would be perfect for a reception following a traditional white wedding. Spread a snowy cloth over the table and polish the silverware till it sparkles. Roll up spotless white napkins and secure with silver ribbon or proper napkin rings. Use silver candlesticks with ivory candles and gilt dishes lined with white napkins or doilies to serve white meringues or white sugared almonds. Fill silver jugs and cut-glass vases with white roses, white sweet peas, lily of the valley and a froth of cow parsley or gypsophila for a table fit for a bride.

When a table will be laden with precious glass and china, the first priority is to check that it's stable, especially if using a folding table or a trestle table. Then spread out an old blanket, baize cloth or proper quilted table protector to prevent splinters from damaging delicate tablecloths, and to cushion glass and china from heavy handling. The tablecloth itself has great decorative potential. Crisp white damask is surprisingly tough and usually shrugs off stains with a thorough wash afterwards. Or make a tablecloth specially for the occasion from upholstery fabric, choosing a design to echo your chosen theme. Stitching it with swags, frills and furbelows will result in a table that rivals the guests themselves for glamour. Hang or sew small weights to the corners of the cloth to prevent it flapping in a breeze.

Finishing touches are vital. There's no need to follow convention for place settings. For example, you could use humble brown card-and-string luggage tags tied to the napkins; or indicate guests' places with tiny boats made from walnut-shell halves or sculpted from pastry, inscribing each name on a paper sail secured with a cocktail-stick mast. If you don't have silver napkin rings, decorate loops of florist's wire with leaves and flowers, or tie napkins with lengths of ribbon or embroidered and beaded braid. It's the detail that makes the difference.

TOP RIGHT: CREATE AN OPULENT TABLE SETTING WITH JEWEL-COLOURED WINE GLASSES. YOU DON'T NEED A MATCHING SET: CONTRASTING COLOURS LIKE RICH GREEN AND GOLD LOOK STUNNING.

TOP, FAR RIGHT: CHOOSE FLOWERS THAT ECHO THE COLOURS OF THE CERAMICS, THE GLASSWARE OR EVEN THE FOOD. HERE, YELLOW ROSES REPEAT THE COLOUR OF THE GLASS BEAKERS, AND THEIR LEAVES MATCH THE PLATES.

BOTTOM RIGHT: A CANDY-STRIPED COFFEE CUP AND A TABLE SCATTERED WITH FRESH PETALS. THE INTENSE PINK BLOSSOM IS THE SAME SHADE AS THE DEEPEST COLOUR ON THE CUP.

BOTTOM, FAR RIGHT: FANCY TAPES, COMPLETE WITH RIBBON FLOWERS AND BEADING, CAN BE DRAPED ACROSS THE TABLE LIKE STREAMERS OR CUT INTO SHORT LENGTHS AND USED TO TIE AROUND NAPKINS.

A MIDSUMMER WEDDING

No wedding is more romantic than one held at midsummer. There's the promise of soft balmy weather, and masses of the most voluptuous garden flowers to be gathered to decorate church and tables, and to be bunched and bound into the bride's and bridesmaids' posies. Tables can be set with the season's finest fruits mounded into pyramids or piled into cut-glass dishes and drifted with the merest whisper of sugar. The wedding party can spill out into the garden and carry on until the moon is high in the sky.

BELOW LEFT: SWEET PEAS ARE ROMANTICALLY FRILLY AND BEAUTIFULLY SCENTED. DON'T BE TEMPTED TO ADD OTHER FLOWERS TO THE VASE WITH THEM AS SWEET PEAS EXUDE MINUTE QUANTITIES OF ETHYLENE THAT MAKE FLOWERS 'TURN' QUICKLY.

RIGHT: A LIGHT, AIRY CANOPY FEELS
MORE SUMMERY THAN A FULL-BLOWN
MARQUEE. MOST MARQUEE COMPANIES
ALSO HIRE OUT CANOPIES, OR THEY CAN
BE BOUGHT IN KIT FORM. REPEATING
FLOWERS AND FOLIAGE FROM THE TABLE
SETTING IN A GARLAND FOR THE CANOPY
COORDINATES THE THEME.

LEFT: VERY YOUNG BRIDESMAIDS WILL
FEEL MORE COMFORTABLE IN SOFT
COTTON JERSEY DRESSES THAN IN
SCRATCHY NET PETTICOATS AND STIFF
TAFFETA. AND THE BETTER THEY FEEL,
THE BETTER THEY SHOULD BEHAVE.

OVERLEAF: AN INFORMAL WEDDING
TABLE MIXES RUSTIC STONEWARE
BOTTLES HOLDING LILY OF THE VALLEY
WITH A MORE ELABORATE TIERED
CENTREPIECE OF WHITE ANEMONES,
WHITE PHLOX, GREENISH-WHITE
GUELDER ROSES AND SPRAYS OF
BLOSSOM. HEART-SHAPED CANDLE
SCREENS ADD TO THE AIR OF ROMANCE.

THE WEDDING PARTY

Preparing as far in advance as possible helps things run smoothly on the big day. Most baking can be done ahead and puddings such as syllabubs and homemade jellies can be made the day before – but you may need to hire an extra refrigerator or borrow space in a neighbour's fridge.

Wedding favours can be wrapped well ahead of the day and made into an eye-catching display from which guests can help themselves on departure. You could fill a tray lined with fragrant leaves – for instance, lemon geranium or eucalyptus – with neatly wrapped miniature bars of luxury scented soap; make a decorative 'tree' by suspending drawstring muslin bags of coloured sweets from a branch securely wedged in a vase or pot; or pile net-and-ribbon packages of sugared almonds on a glass compote.

On the wedding morning, set the table with china, silverware and flowers, and make a final check for stray leaves and insects, as well as fallen petals, just before the guests arrive.

In the book *Cold Comfort Farm*, Stella Gibbons's early 20th-century comedy of manners, Elfine, one of the Starkadder family, is married on Midsummer's Day: 'Midsummer Day dawned with a thick grey haze in the air and a heavy dew on the meadow and trees... Flora noted the heat-haze with joy. It would be a day of heat; brilliant, blue and radiant... The awning was up, looking immediately festive, as awnings always do. And in the kitchen the two long trestle tables were decorated and ready... there were syllabubs, ice-pudding, caviar sandwiches, crab patties, trifle, and champagne.' Who could wish for more?

BELOW LEFT: SET ASIDE A TABLE TO HOLD GIFTS AS THEY ARE PRESENTED AND THEY CAN BECOME PART OF THE DISPLAY TOO.

BELOW: MAKE A FEATURE OF AFTER-DINNER BOTTLES OF SPIRITS IN VARYING SIZES, CHILLING THEM ON CHUNKS OF ICE IN A SIMPLE BOWL.

RIGHT: HAVE SUCCESSIVE STAGES OF THE FEAST WAITING IN THE WINGS: HERE, TEACUPS, CUPCAKES AND HOMEMADE MERINGUES IN A GLASS CONFECTIONERY JAR STAND READY TO BE BROUGHT TO THE TABLE.

BELOW: A DEFT WRAPPING OF LEAVES CONCEALS A BLOCK OF FLORIST'S FOAM THAT HOLDS AN ARRANGEMENT OF ROSES AND BORAGE FLOWERS.

LEFT: A BRIDESMAID'S 'POSY' OF PURE WHITE ANEMONES IN A HUMBLE JAM JAR TIED WITH TWINE. A TABLESPOON OF WATER IN THE JAR KEEPS FLOWERS FRESH FOR A FEW HOURS.

BELOW LEFT: PINK MOPHEAD HYDRANGEAS MAKE AN UNUSUAL POSY AND HAVE THE GREAT ADVANTAGE OF BEING THORN-FREE.

BELOW: PINK ROSES WITH CONTRASTING IVY BERRIES MAKE A SOPHISTICATED BOUQUET AS WELL AS BRINGING GOOD LUCK FOR THE BRIDE. IN THE VICTORIAN 'LANGUAGE OF FLOWERS', ROSES SYMBOLIZE LOVE AND PASSION, WHILE IVY REPRESENTS FAITHFULNESS.

BELOW RIGHT: A MODEST DAISY CHAIN MAKES A CHARMING AND INFORMAL BRIDESMAID'S CIRCLET THAT IS GOSSAMER-LIGHT TO WEAR. RED ROSES BEHIND THE EARS ADD UNEXPECTED PANACHE.

WEDDING FLOWERS

A country wedding at the height of summer gives you every chance to cut and arrange the flowers yourself or to ask friends and neighbours to help. Roses and sweet peas, the most sweetly scented and romantic of flowers, are at their flowering peak, along with plenty of greenery to encircle posies and trim tables.

Flowers should echo the tone of the occasion and reflect its location. The architecture of the church is important: simple wildflowers will suit a humble village chapel, while grander churches demand more formal flowers. The setting for the wedding will influence your choice, as, of course, will the bride's dress. White is still the classic shade for a wedding, but for more unusual alternatives, take an unprejudiced look around the garden and use your imagination.

In *Cold Comfort Farm*, for Elfine's wedding the small country church was all decked out in white using cottage garden favourites: 'So the pews were hung with chains of marguerites, and two tall lilies stood like archangelic trumpets at the end of each pew, lining the aisle. There were many jars filled with white pinks, and the altar steps where the bride would kneel were banked with snowy geraniums.'

Bridesmaids always fidget, so their posies must be securely bound to make a firm handle, perhaps with an extra ribbon loop to be slipped over the wrist; or give them tiny baskets, with a block of florist's foam packed with flower heads. For utter rustic simplicity, let them carry a jam jar of flowers held by a twine handle.

A DAY AT THE BEACH

The long summer holidays would hardly be complete without a day at the beach. Children relish the chance to swim or paddle and build sandcastles, while grown-ups are overcome with nostalgia for Thermos flasks of stewed tea and sandwiches with an extra seasoning of sand. Even the most technology-conscious children still clamour for a bucket and spade when a trip to the beach is planned.

To enjoy a day at the seaside with children means planning ahead. Things can take a turn for the worse if sun hats and sunscreens are left behind or someone forgets the rubber rings. Older members of the party may appreciate an inflatable cushion, an airbed or a folding chair. Lack of shade is always a problem on the beach: a giant garden parasol or a simple canopy will help shield the midday sun, while a pop-up play tent will entice children under cover from time to time.

RIGHT: A HOME-MADE CANOPY SHIELDS FIERCE SUNLIGHT AND ITS GUY ROPES ARE IDEAL FOR DRYING WET TOWELS AND COSTUMES. A FOLDING PICNIC TABLE KEEPS SAND OUT OF THE SANDWICHES.

BELOW LEFT AND BELOW: KEEP FOOD SIMPLE – IT WILL TASTE GOOD WHATEVER YOU SERVE. MOST DEPARTMENT STORES SELL BRIGHTLY COLOURED UNBREAKABLE PICNICWARE.

LEFT: DIGGING IN THE SAND MAY YIELD BURIED TREASURE – OR AN ANGRY RAGWORM, A RAZOR SHELL OR A COCKLE OR TWO.

BELOW: OLD-FASHIONED TIN BUCKETS ARE PERFECT FOR HOLDING BEACHCOMBING FINDS.

BELOW RIGHT: PAPER PARASOLS ARE CHEAP AND PRETTY, AND THEY ARE A CLEVER WAY OF KEEPING THE SUN OFF CHILDREN – IF ONLY FOR A SHORT TIME.

OVERLEAF: ENJOYING THE FREEDOM OF AN EMPTY STRETCH OF SAND, SEA AND SKY.

BEACH ACTIVITIES

Have a battery of ideas ready to keep children amused. Beachcombing walks along high tide mark yield all sorts of treasures: leathery mermaid's purses (the egg cases of the dogfish), crab claws, dry clusters of empty whelk's eggs or occasionally a giant jellyfish stranded by the tide. Picking up seaweed usually disturbs clouds of sand-hoppers or the odd sea slater. Popping the air pockets on dried bladderwrack is every bit as satisfying as bursting plastic bubblewrap. Let children take home a piece of seaweed – bladderwrack is ideal – to help them become amateur weather forecasters. When the seaweed is crisp and dry, the weather will be fine; when it is limp and damp, rain is on its way. (The secret is that the seaweed is hygroscopic and so absorbs humidity from the air.)

All over the beach there are shells, glass fragments polished by the waves and pebbles to be collected. They can be taken home and used to decorate flower pots, frames and boxes for pretty homemade seaside souvenirs. When beachcombing palls, organize a competition to build the biggest sandcastle, or umpire a game of beach cricket, softball, volleyball or soccer. Playing catch with a ball or frisbie or flying a kite are other activities that are tailormade for sandy beaches.

EXPLORING ROCKPOOLS

When the tide is at its lowest ebb, exploring the exposed rocks can be positively educational. Limpets are easily spotted above the waterline: their conical shells resemble Chinese coolie hats and are immovably welded to the rock while the tide is out. Alongside, you may find encrustations of grey barnacles, firmly closed against the drying action of the air. (If your knowledge of the seashore is shaky, borrow a guidebook from the library to identify finds.)

Pools between the rocks are home to various species of crabs. One of the most charming is the hermit crab, which appropriates an empty winkle or whelk shell to protect its soft body. Sea anemones above the waterline look like blobs of jelly attached to the rocks: underwater, they put out delicate tentacles and reveal their pretty beaded patterns. Children may also find starfish and brittle-stars and, in deeper pools, prawns and small fish. Seaweeds that look unprepossessingly slimy flattened against a rock will fan out into ferny, lacy patterns in water.

Encourage children to respect sea life by carefully replacing any stones they have lifted, without crushing creatures underneath, and by returning crabs, starfish and other temporary captives to their pools after they've studied them at close quarters.

Local newspapers list the times of high and low tide. As soon as the tide reaches its lowest ebb, it starts to creep back in again, but the extent of the rocky beach will affect how much time you get to explore. Keep an eye on the open sea all the while children are absorbed in the rock pools: the tide can turn with astonishing speed.

LEFT: IF CHILDREN CAN BE PERSUADED TO SIT STILL, OFTEN THE BEST IDEA IS TO WAIT AND WATCH WHILE A ROCK POOL GRADUALLY REVEALS ITS SECRET LIFE.

BELOW: CRAB-RACING IS FUN. THERE'S AN ART TO AVOIDING NIPPED FINGERS BUT NO WAY OF ENSURING THAT THE CRABS PLAY FAIR. ALWAYS PUT THE CRABS BACK WHERE YOU FOUND THEM WHEN THE RACE IS OVER.

Greet guests arriving at a garden party or wedding feast with a celebratory glass of kir. Pour a dash of crème de cassis into each glass and top up with chilled sparkling wine (there's no point in using the best champagne). Adding a few fresh blackcurrants to each glass will intensify the flavour. Delicious variations include substituting crème de mûres (blackberries) or framboises (raspberries) for the blackcurrant liqueur.

If you want napkins in a particular shade to complete a table setting, it's easy to make your own. Buy some coloured linen and cut it into 50cm (20in) squares for generously sized napkins. Turn under the raw edges twice to create narrow double hems, mitring the corners for a neat finish, then stitch. For a final touch, embellish the napkins with simple embroidery stitches such as French knots, blanket stitch, star filling stitch and running stitch (all shown here). Other simple stitches such as chain stitch and cross stitch would also look good.

Fresh rose petals make the most extravagantly romantic confetti, especially if you gather them from sweetly scented varieties. For perfumed perfection, pick the flowers with the dew still on them on the morning of the wedding, then carefully strip off the petals and pack them into pretty boxes. The vicar will be pleased too, as rose petals are biodegradable and won't leave the churchyard looking as if it is strewn with litter.

Use beaded covers to keep cream, sugar and drinks insect-free when laying tables in advance out of doors. Cut two circles of linen or muslin and stitch them together, with right sides facing, leaving a small gap. Turn right side out and stitch the gap closed, then press flat. Or you can simply hem a square of fabric. Use embroidery thread to attach the beads around the edge: make a loop every 2.5cm (1in), thread on a bead then backstitch to secure the loop in place. Alternatively, buy beads ready-stitched to cotton tape, and sew lengths onto the covers.

As the celebration draws to a close, hand out party favours to say thank you for coming. They needn't be expensive – a handful of sweets in a generous square of net or chiffon tied up with a curly paper streamer makes a pretty memento. Heap them in a glass dish or on a fruit stand, ready to hand to guests as they leave.

This storm lantern has a deep kick-up, or well, to hold the candle steady, making it ideal for holding a layer of water on which flowers are floating. There's no reason why the same trick shouldn't work equally well in an ordinary glass jar, as long as the candle is firmly fixed to the base with molten wax or glue. Use individual flowers such as hydrangea florets, busy lizzies (Impatiens) or phlox.

A length of rich velvet ribbon or a bow of hazy gauze will make your gift stand out from the rest. Buy ribbon by the metre (yard) from a haberdashery (notions) shop or a department store and practise tying it until you are satisfied with how it looks. Wrapping the present in plain-coloured handmade paper will maximize the ribbon's impact.

When there are children around, picnic food is best served in unbreakable plastic dishes. Picnicware and food containers have become more and more stylish in recent years, and high street shops produce new ranges every summer with bowls, beakers, plates and Thermos flasks in coordinating bright colours – there's no excuse for packing up a picnic in tired old sandwich boxes or tatty empty ice-cream cartons.

Paper rosebuds sold as cake decorations make dainty and inexpensive napkin rings that are almost as pretty as the real thing – and are guaranteed to last a bit longer. They come on a short length of wire that's just long enough to be shaped into a semicircle to hold a rolled napkin loosely in place. If you can bear to sacrifice real rosebuds, cut them with a very short stem and create an artificial flexible stem with a length of florist's wire, bound with green florist's tape.

Use beachcombing finds of shells and glass fragments polished smooth by the waves to decorate a mirror set in a frame with a deep border. The delicate design pictured needs only a handful of shells, but if you've brought back a bucketful, the frame will look equally attractive encrusted with shells and pebbles so that no scrap of background is visible. Plan your design first by laying the shells in position; fix them in their final arrangement with strong clear adhesive.

A windbreak can spell the difference between enjoying and enduring a day at the beach. Approximately 4m (4yd) of tough canvas will make a generous screen; five sturdy canes are slotted into casings in the fabric. At each end, turn under 1cm (½in) and then turn under by the required width of the casing plus 6mm (¼in); stitch 6mm (¼in) from the turned-under edge. Mark pencil or chalk lines on the wrong side dividing the canvas into quarters. For each casing, fold along one line, right sides facing, and stitch parallel to the line, the width of the casing away from it. Slot in the canes, roll up the windbreak and you're ready to go.

A circle of fresh foliage makes an elegant napkin ring. Creepers and climbing plants have naturally pliant stems that can be bent into shape. Here a cutting from a grapevine with leaves and tendrils attached has been used; other garden alternatives include ivy, jasmine and hops. Join stem ends by binding them with florist's wire, and lay napkins join-side down.

Create an outdoor summer dining room with folding chairs and picnic tables. Folding furniture is easy to move around, it takes up much less space when it's stored for the winter and it is also useful if you want to take some furniture on a picnic. Add touches that you wouldn't normally consider doing outside, such as a vase of flowers. In a rural setting, an assortment of junk-shop furniture and flea-market finds can look more appropriate than a matching dining set from the garden centre.

A flower-petal salad is a quintessential summer dish that can be prepared only when the garden is in full bloom. Edible flowers include marigolds (Calendula), roses and nasturtiums, plus herbs in bloom such as chives, thyme, mint, fennel and starry blue borage. Start with a base of lettuce leaves in a shallow dish, then scatter with the flowers. Serve with a suitably flowery vinaigrette that's had a drop or two of rose water added.

Punctuate the dusk at evening parties with hanging nightlights (votives). Use glass flower pots or jam jars and make handles for them from pliable galvanized wire (from hardware shops). First cut a length of wire a little longer than the circumference of the jar. Then cut a length for the handle and twist each end into a loop. Thread the first length through each loop and wrap around the jar just below the lip or rim. Twist the cut ends together until the wire grips the jam jar tightly, then bend back the twisted join neatly against the jar.

Sugared almonds are traditional wedding favours. Instead of wrapping them in a circle of net, make paper cones that will hold a handful or two; folding down and fastening the top will stop them from spilling out. Decorate the cones with ribbon bows, paper flowers or streamers. Look out for gold and silvered almonds, as well as the more familiar pastel colours.

Autumn

Harvest Festival

Celebrating the harvest is a ritual that dates back to pagan times, when people gave thanks to the corn spirit for a good crop and special rituals were performed to ensure a successful crop the following year. People believed that the 'spirit' of the corn – or of whichever grain they were harvesting – resided in the crop itself and would die when the last stalks were cut unless certain procedures were followed. The responsibility for cutting the last stand of corn was often shared, so the burden shouldn't fall on any one person.

In many places in Britain and Europe, the last sheaf was dressed in women's clothing, bedecked with ribbons and flowers and honoured as harvest doll or queen. It was carried with ceremony to preside over the harvest home or supper and hung in the barn to supervise threshing, before spending the winter in the farmhouse. In spring the grains rubbed from the ears were either sown with new grain or fed to the plough horse to restore the corn spirit to the land.

Making corn dollies and plaiting straw into decorative cornucopia, fans, horseshoes, sheaves and wreaths is a vestige of these ancient rituals. Present-day cultivars of corn make the task difficult – long-stemmed hollow straw gives best results but these are undesirable traits in the field and have been bred out of modern strains.

ABOVE LEFT: MUCH OF THE HARD LABOUR OF HARVEST HAS DISAPPEARED WITH MODERN MECHANIZATION.

LEFT: ALTHOUGH OUR FOREBEARS WOULD HARDLY RECOGNIZE THESE OUTSIZE BALES, THERE'S STILL SOMETHING INHERENTLY ROMANTIC ABOUT WHILING AWAY AN AFTERNOON IN THE SHADE OF WHAT APPROXIMATES TO A MODERN HAY-RICK.

RIGHT: A CHURCH SPIRE FLOATING ABOVE FIELDS OF GOLDEN STUBBLE. THE CHURCH RATHER THAN THE FARM IS NOW THE MAIN FOCUS FOR HARVEST CELEBRATIONS.

BRINGING IN THE HARVEST

The harvest was a family affair, with everyone roped in to lend a hand; children's long summer holidays from school are a direct link with our agricultural past, when they were expected to help bring the crop in. It was not only a family affair but a neighbourly one, too.

'It was the custom, if the farmer hadna much strength about him,' wrote Mary Webb in *Precious Bane*, 'that he should fix on a day for the neighbours to come and give him a hand in the lugging of the grain.' In this tale of early-19th-century country life (published in the 1920s) she describes what a great and cheerful occasion it was, and how even the horses and wagons were decked out for the harvest. 'It was very early when the waggons began to roll into the fold, with a solemn, gladsome sound, and each with his own pair of horses or oxen. Each farmer brought his own men and his own waggon, and sometimes he brought two. The teams were decked out with ribbons and flowers, and some had a motto as well, such as "Luck to our Day" or "God Bless the Corn".'

The church obviously acknowledged the importance of the harvest to the survival of the community. A peal of bells often announced the last loaded wagon as it arrived safely in the farmyard. In some villages the crop was blessed by the priest and the corn dolly was even hung on the church door. Harvest time began at Lammas, the name of which comes from the old Saxon word *Llaf-maesse*, or loaf mass, a reference to the grain needed to bake bread. Traditionally Lammas falls on August 1st, and in some country churches a small loaf made from the very first of the newly harvested grain was brought to be blessed.

The Reformation frowned on and outlawed such practices, however, and the church service we know today as harvest festival really dates from 1843. This was when the vicar of Morwenstow in Devon invited his flock to take communion with bread baked from the new corn to celebrate the harvest. Above his own harvest table the vicar would hang a sheaf of corn, which he described as 'the harvest wave-offering, presented at the altar and waved before the Lord at the Harvest Festival'. From this point the festival developed to embrace decorating the church with produce from fields and orchards, and subsequently distributing the donated food to local people in need.

In North America, Thanksgiving Day grew from the harvest festival. The first was held in autumn 1621, when the Pilgrim Fathers – who had set sail from England in the previous year and had established a farming community in present-day Massachusetts – proclaimed a day of thanksgiving for their very first harvest. Later that century, the custom became an annual event in Massachusetts and also in Connecticut, and then in 1865 President Lincoln made Thanksgiving a national holiday. It now takes place on the fourth Thursday of November and is the biggest family celebration of the year in North America.

ABOVE LEFT: NEWLY CUT CORN SHAPED
INTO MINI-SHEAVES AND TIED WITH
RAFFIA, PLUS A HANDFUL OF APPLES, IS SET
AMONG THE MORE CUSTOMARY CHURCH
DECORATIONS.

LEFT: BASKETS OF 'COOKERS' AND
'EATERS'. EVERY CROP IS CELEBRATED
AT THE HARVEST FESTIVAL, NOT JUST
THE CORN.

RIGHT: GIFTS OF FLOWERS AND FRUIT
LEFT AT THE CHURCH DOOR WILL BE USED
TO DECORATE THE FONT, WINDOW-SILLS,
SCREEN AND BALCONY OF A SMALL
VILLAGE CHURCH.

ℋARVEST SUPPER

THIS PAGE, BELOW: FOOD FOR THE HARVEST SUPPER MUST SATISFY HEARTY APPETITES AFTER A LONG DAY WORKING IN THE FIELDS. (LEFT) A PROPER CRUSTY LOAF. (CENTRE) A LATTICE PIE WITH A SEASONAL APPLE AND BLACKBERRY FILLING. (RIGHT) A RUSTIC WOODEN TRAY HOLDING NAPKINS, CUTLERY AND A TRADITIONAL STONEWARE MUG.

OPPOSITE, BELOW: (LEFT) A BOWL OF LOCAL APPLES IN ALL SHAPES AND SIZES THAT WOULD NEVER PLEASE A SUPERMARKET BUYER BUT CAN'T BE BEATEN FOR TASTE AND FLAVOUR. (CENTRE) A CRATE OF MARROWS WAITING TO BE TURNED INTO CHUTNEYS AND RELISHES. (RIGHT) BREAD AND STRONG CHEESE – A PLOUGHMAN'S LUNCH OR A HARVESTER'S SUPPER.

OPPOSITE, ABOVE: TO FINISH OFF, AN APPLE TART WITH CREAM AND A MUG OF COFFEE BY CANDLELIGHT.

OVERLEAF: A REAL HARVEST HOME SET OUT IN THE FIELDS, THOUGH NOT ON THE SCALE OF THOSE HELD BACK IN THE PRE-MECHANIZATION DAYS.

Before the days of combine harvesters, the harvest supper, or 'harvest home', began as soon as the last laden wagon rolled into the farmyard. As it came to a halt, a great shout went up and the reapers burst into a traditional chorus: 'We have ploughed, we have sowed/We have reaped, we have mowed/We have brought home every load/Hip Hip Hip – Harvest Home!'

Then the feasting began in earnest to celebrate the harvest safely gathered in. It was the one time in the year when everyone sat down together, farmer alongside labourer, all united by a hard day's work.

In Mary Webb's *Precious Bane*, the feast was laid out ready in the orchard: 'We'd got fifty people coming, no less, counting the women-folk. I was up afore dawn getting all ready, setting the china, both ours and what we'd borrowed, on the trestles in the orchard, helping Gideon to put the casks of beer in the yard, ready for the men to fill their harvest bottles, and fetching water from the well for the tea. The orchard was a sight to see when the trestles were set out (for I could put all ready with no fear of rain on such a day) with the mugs and platters of many colours, and the brown quartern loaves, and the big pats of butter stamped with a swan, and the slabs of honeycomb dough cakes, gingerbread, cheese, jam and jelly, let alone the ham at one end of the trestle and the round of beef at the other.'

And after the feast, there were games and dancing and singing – particularly drinking songs: 'Then drink, boys, drink!/And see ye do not spill,/For if ye do, ye shall drink two,/For 'tis our master's will.' Which no doubt encouraged the singers' hands to tremble as they held their pint pots.

Today, now that far fewer people are involved in bringing in the harvest, the harvest supper exists in a different form but has not been abandoned altogether; instead, it has become more closely linked with the church service. The supper is organized by parishioners rather than farm workers, and sometimes tickets are sold to raise money for church funds or charity. But the purpose remains the same – to celebrate and give thanks for the harvest.

Whether you live in a farming community or in the city, it is still satisfying to mark this time of year with your own harvest supper, served country-style, for family and friends. Food should be hearty, robust and, above all, plentiful. Stick to seasonal produce and choose dishes full of country flavours. If you feel adventurous, try your hand at baking a traditional harvest loaf in the shape of a corn sheaf. (Or you may find a baker willing to produce such a loaf for you.)

Harvest suppers were traditionally laid out on long tables in barns. Decorate your room, or barn if you are fortunate enough to have access to one, with swags of corn, wreaths of grasses and grains (see pages 82–3) and baskets of rosy apples or gourds. You could even use hollowed-out pumpkins as tureens to hold soup or snacks. Set jugs of cottage garden flowers and carafes of fruit cordial and country wine or cider along the table. Traditional salt-glazed vessels, such as the mug shown on the tray below left, were known as harvestware and were made for over 200 years for farm workers to take to the fields with their harvest bottles – if you can find any of this tableware, it would make a perfect addition to your harvest table. The finishing touch would be to arrange for a group of musicians to play country-style music after the meal, to encourage the celebrations to continue through the evening and into the small hours.

HARVEST WREATHS

In some European countries, the finest ears of corn from the last sheaf to be harvested were woven into a wreath and entwined with flowers. The prettiest girl in the village then wore the wreath to the farmhouse and the farmer hung it up in the hall. The following Sunday, he took it to the church to be blessed and then he kept it until Easter, when grain from the wreath was scattered in among the newly sprouted corn – a similar tradition to that of sowing the old corn along with the new or feeding it to the plough horse.

Wreaths of corn make ideal decorations for harvest-festival or harvest supper celebrations, without paying too much heed to earlier superstition. To make a modern-day wreath, start with a base of thick-gauge galvanized wire looped into a substantial circle three strands thick. Gather together a selection of grasses and grains such as corn, wheat, oats, fox-tail millet and quaking-grass, and tie the grasses into small neat bunches, preferably with natural-coloured raffia. Use more lengths of raffia to tie the bunches of grass to the wire wreath, working in one direction with the seedheads all lying the same way and overlapping the stalks. When the wreath is densely covered, you can add smooth grey poppy seedheads for contrast, plus small sunflower heads with the dried yellow petals still attached. Attach a raffia loop to hold the wreath and hang it where you will.

When the wreaths are no longer needed indoors or start to look a little past their best, they still have a role to perform: hang them outside for a treat for seed-eating birds such as sparrows and finches.

ABOVE LEFT: GATHER MEADOW AND GARDEN GRASSES TO MAKE YOUR OWN HARVEST WREATHS, OR BUY STEMS READY-DRIED FROM SPECIALIST FLOWER SHOPS. YOU CAN BUY SPRAYS OF MILLET, FOR EXAMPLE, IN PET SHOPS.

LEFT AND RIGHT: SUPPLEMENT GRASSES WITH HOME-GROWN POPPY SEEDHEADS AND SUNFLOWER HEADS. IF THE WEATHER IS FINE, SIMPLY LEAVE THEM TO RIPEN ON THE PLANT; IF NOT, BRING THEM INDOORS TO DRY OUT. (DON'T HANG POPPY SEEDHEADS UPSIDE DOWN TO DRY OR YOU'LL END UP WITH SEEDS DROPPING ALL OVER THE FLOOR.)

WOODLAND WALKS

Celebrate autumn's bounty with a walk through the woods as the season gives way to winter in a blaze of glory. There are sloes and damsons to gather and steep in gin for Christmas liqueurs; clusters of hazelnuts to be pulled down with a stout stick; and the last handfuls of blackberries. (But don't pick the blackberries after Michaelmas Day, September 29th, when the Devil is said to have spat on them.)

For cheerful colour around the house, bring back sprays of rose-hips and haws, two-tone spindle berries, and skeins of 'old man's beard' (wild clematis) with its soft, fluffy seedheads. In some places, wild hop-bines tangled through the hedges can be carefully unravelled and brought home to garland a mantelpiece, lintel or beam. Alternatively, order one by post; its heady scent will permeate the house and, according to plant lore, ensure that everyone sleeps soundly.

FAR LEFT: EVEN IF YOU STROLL NO FURTHER THAN THE GARDEN GATE, YOU CAN FIND PLENTY OF PLANTS WITH AUTUMN COLOUR TO CUT FOR THE HOUSE. PYRACANTHA BERRIES ARE IDEAL – LONG-LASTING AND DENSELY CLUSTERED.

BELOW: MICHAELMAS DAISIES OFTEN GROW WILD. THEY ARE ONE OF THE LATEST SPECIES TO FLOWER AND ARE ALL THE MORE WELCOME FOR THAT.

LEFT: AUTUMN BOUNTY, INCLUDING BEECH AND SMOKE BUSH (COTINUS) LEAVES, PLUS CRAB APPLES, PYRACANTHA AND COTONEASTER BERRIES.

LEFT: A MUSHROOM PICKER'S WALKING STICK IS A USEFUL IDIOSYNCRASY – A WOVEN CANE BASKET WITH A STURDY WOODEN WALKING STICK INSERTED THROUGH THE MIDDLE.

RIGHT: A TRUFFLE HUNTER AND HIS DOG WORK ALMOST EMPATHETICALLY, WITH ONLY THE QUIETEST WORDS OF PRAISE TO ENCOURAGE THE DOG. IN FRANCE, SOME HUNTERS PREFER TO TRAIN A PIG TO FIND THE TRUFFLES.

FAR RIGHT, TOP: ALONG WITH CAVIAR, TRUFFLES ARE THE MOST EXPENSIVE FOOD IN THE WORLD. THE ELUSIVE WHITE TRUFFLE, SHOWN HERE, IS THE RAREST OF ALL AND IS PRICED ACCORDINGLY – IN EXCESS OF £1,000 A KILO ($725 A POUND), DEPENDING ON THE ANNUAL HARVEST. WHITE TRUFFLES ARE SO PRECIOUS THAT THEY ARE BEST EATEN RAW, IN FINE SHAVINGS SCATTERED OVER PASTA DRESSED WITH NOTHING BUT BUTTER.

MUSHROOMS AND TRUFFLES

On dew-drenched autumn mornings there are field mushrooms to be picked for breakfast – sublime just fried in butter and served on toast. There are a whole host of different fungi that are equally delicious: horse mushrooms and fresh puffballs before they turn to dust and, from woods and forests, apricot-coloured chanterelles, violet-capped blewits, parasols and shaggy caps. Funnel-shaped horns of plenty often grow in clusters in beech woods and can be gathered and dried for winter use, as can various species of brown-capped boletus, which also show a preference for beech trees.

In rural France there's nothing more natural than for the whole family to go on a mushroom hunt equipped with wicker baskets. In other regions, where few people possess the detailed knowledge to identify edible species with absolute confidence, help is at hand. Scanning the local press at this time of year will

usually turn up a proper organized fungi foray, led by experts who will confirm the edibility (or otherwise) of everything you pick.

Delicious as a dish of chanterelles cooked with butter, cream and garlic is, there is still one fungus that outshines them all – the incomparable truffle. For a few short weeks each year, truffle hunters in Italy and France set out with their prize dogs to track down fungi worth their weight in gold. In Italy, Piedmont is the main truffle-hunting region; in France, it is Périgord. Truffles grow on tree roots – especially oaks – and the hunters must train their dogs to sniff them out up to 30cm (1ft) underground and then to dig until commanded to stop. The smallest specimens are not gathered but carefully covered up and left to mature for up to seven years. Hunters need a photographic memory – to find the same site again years later on the forest floor is no mean feat. Not surprisingly, they are fiercely protective of their hounds and of the area they search.

ABOVE: BLACK TRUFFLES ON SALE IN A MARKET IN THE PÉRIGORD REGION OF FRANCE. THESE TRUFFLES ARE PRIZED FOR THE DEPTH OF FLAVOUR THAT EVEN A SMALL SLICE WILL ADD TO A DISH.

H ALLOWEEN

Halloween, the eve of All Hallows or All Saints' Day, was once the ancient Celtic New Year's Eve, when thanks were given to the sun god for the harvest, and Samhain, lord of death, was celebrated at the dying of the year. It was a night of black magic, when witches, ghosts and spirits of the dead returned to earth. Great bonfires wre lit to ward off witches but also to welcome the ghosts of ancestors. Lanterns carved from mangel-wurzels (a large kind of beet) and turnips kept evil spirits at bay.

When the Romans invaded Britain, they brought with them the festival of Pomona, held to honour the goddess of fruit. As both celebrations were held on the same day, they gradually merged over the years. Many traditional Halloween games still played today in fact have their roots in the Roman festival. In duck apple, or bobbing for apples, apples are floated in a tub of water and contestants have to try to pick up one in their teeth – good luck awaits whoever succeeds. In snap-apple, the fruits are hung from string on a wooden pole and again the aim is to get your teeth into one. An even older and more dangerous version had a stick with an apple on one end and a lighted candle on the other suspended from a pole. A circle of children stood round and tried to bite the apple as it swung in their direction.

Halloween was a propitious time for trying to predict the future. If you combed your hair at midnight while eating an apple and gazing into a mirror, a vision of your future partner was thought to appear in the glass. Women would go into the fields to sow hemp seed, chanting, 'Hemp seed I sow, who will be my husband, let him come and mow.' A backward glance over the left shoulder was meant to reveal the man they would marry. And girls with a sweetheart would throw a hazelnut into the fire and say, 'If he loves me, pop and fly. If he hates me, lie and die.'

LEFT TOP: In the past lanterns tended to be carved from mangel-wurzels and turnips, but today pumpkins and squashes offer far more scope. Don't feel obliged to use a perfectly spherical golden globe. Turn the page to see how a curious 'Turk's turban' squash like this makes an unusual lantern.

LEFT BOTTOM: Ripe and unripe pumpkins lie partly hidden on the ground beneath the large protective leaves of the plant.

RIGHT: All kinds of squashes and pumpkins can be turned into lanterns – don't overlook the smaller varieties. Use white 'patty pan' and grey 'crown prince' squashes to make companion lanterns to a giant globe, pictured here on a market stall in France.

JACK-O'-LANTERNS

In many areas, people would get dressed up at Halloween and blacken their faces with soot or put on a mask, then go from house to house asking for food and money. Known as guisers (from disguisers), they often carried turnip masks and lanterns, a relic of the old Celtic festival of Samhain. Their modern counterparts are children, wearing costumes and masks, going from door to door to demand 'Trick or treat'. Householders usually prefer to hand over sweets rather than risk falling victim to a trick.

Making lanterns from pumpkins, and to a lesser extent from squashes, marrows and turnips, has been elevated from hacking out a crude spooky face into something of a folk art. While children still love to carve a fierce face on a pumpkin to grin from the window-sill on Halloween, adults can indulge in more creative lantern-making. Collecting together a few tools will make the job easier: a lino-cutting tool with its grooved blade is ideal for cutting straight lines; a gimlet makes perfect small holes; a flat-edged wood-carving tool is useful for lifting out areas of skin without piercing the pumpkin; and a craft knife is best for cutting out shapes.

Before you start, make sure the pumpkin has a flat base – shave a piece off if necessary so that it sits firmly. Slice off the top to make a lid, and then start scooping out the seeds and flesh. Dry the seeds and save them to plant next year or to scatter on the bird table throughout the winter. Or if you like, you can wash off any clinging strands of flesh, dry the seeds and toast them in the oven to serve as a snack. Use the bigger chunks of flesh that you scoop out to make soup or traditional pumpkin pie, or roast them in the oven with butter and black pepper. For a long-lasting lantern, scoop out as much flesh as you can to leave a thin outer shell. You'll get more light from the lantern – the whole pumpkin will appear to glow – and it won't go mouldy quite so quickly.

A combination of pierced designs and areas where the pumpkin skin has been lifted but the flesh remains will give a variation in intensity of light. If you don't feel sufficiently confident to carve your chosen design freehand, trace it on first using a child's washable felt pen so that you can wipe away any guidelines when you've finished cutting.

Nightlights (votives) are perfect to place inside jack-o'-lanterns – taller candles are not so stable and would burn the pumpkin lid if you wanted to use one.

RIGHT: TURNING A TURK'S TURBAN SQUASH INTO A LANTERN PRESENTS MORE OF A CHALLENGE – THIS ONE MAKES A FEATURE OF ITS KNUCKLED BASE. AN ADDITIONAL LANTERN, MADE BY SLASHING A SMALL GREEN SQUASH AT INTERVALS FROM TOP TO BASE, HAS BEEN BALANCED ON TOP. ITS NEIGHBOUR IS A CLASSIC GOLDEN PUMPKIN, INSCRIBED WITH CURLICUES AND STARS.

OVERLEAF: A GROUP OF GRINNING JACK-O'-LANTERNS CUT FROM GREEN GOURDS IS FLANKED BY POMEGRANATES USED AS CANDLE HOLDERS.

Make a cheerful autumnal buttonhole for a favourite tweed jacket. Pick up the brightest autumn leaves you can find and add a sprig of heather for good luck. Bind the stems with twine and use a safety pin to fasten them to a lapel. The buttonhole will last for days.

Simple is best: tie bundles of corn into mini-sheaves using florist's wire, and arrange them in pairs, stems crossed. Here they've been used to decorate the top of the church organ for harvest festival but would be equally appropriate on a rustic refectory table for harvest supper.

On autumn walks collect 'old man's beard' (wild clematis) and coloured leaves and hang them upside down to dry before using them in indoor arrangements. Add bunches of Chinese lanterns (Physalis) from the garden, plus late chillies from the greenhouse. An old-fashioned clothes-horse makes an ideal drying rack.

Always nail horseshoes this way up for decoration so that the luck doesn't run out. This horseshoe on a shed door has been used to hang a budgie's millet wreath to feed wild birds – sparrows and other seed eaters will appreciate it just as much. A scrap of red raffia to tie it on looks suitably jolly.

For miniature versions of Halloween pumpkin lanterns, try making these tiny pepper lights. Cut off the tops of the peppers, scoop out the seeds and pierce holes in the sides to hold knotted string handles. Add a chilli 'tassel' for extra decoration. Put nightlights (votives) inside the peppers to illuminate them, and then string them through bushes beside the path to greet visitors.

Feed the birds in style with half a coconut filled with a handful of stripy seeds. Use a handsaw to halve the coconut and to make three grooves in the shell to hold the string. Take three lengths of string and knot them together at one end; place the knot under the shell and guide the three lengths of string into the grooves. Fill the coconut with seeds and hang it outside.

A speckled squash or marrow makes a nice upright lantern. Scoop out the seeds and flesh (you can dry the seeds for the birds and save the flesh for making soup) and cut out basic shapes with an ordinary kitchen knife. Use thick natural twine to hang the lantern: the weight of the squash would cause thin, synthetic string to slice right through the flesh.

More stylish ways to feed the birds. Make up a mixture of oats, bacon scraps, nuts, raisins, seeds and breadcrumbs bound together with melted lard, and push the mixture into the crevices in pine cones or large decorative seed pods. Try updating the classic string of monkey nuts by alternating them with dried apricots, hazelnuts and almonds, using a darning needle and wool to thread them. Hang all bird feeders out of reach of cats and other predators.

How do you tell the difference between a pumpkin and a squash? Although they are closely related, pumpkins tend to be spherical or oval and reliably yellow-orange in colour, while squashes are far more varied in both shape and colour. This lantern, quite clearly, is carved from a pumpkin.

Dried lavender is a legacy of summer. Cut the stems in full flower and hang them in bunches to dry in a cool, dark cupboard. If you don't have time to strip the flowers and sew them into classic lavender bags, simply trim the stems, tie them into mini-sheaves and arrange them in a basket on a shelf, table or window-sill. Gently squeeze a bunch every time you pass by and wait for a fragrant blast of summer to assail your nostrils.

Line up early varieties of pears and apples to ripen at a sunny window. Or put them in a bowl with a ripe tomato: the ethylene the tomato gives off will help the fruit to ripen. Alternatively, wrap pears in brown paper and leave them in a dark cupboard for a few days to speed up the ripening process. The traditional way to store apples and pears throughout the winter is to lay them in shallow boxes, stacked in a frost-free attic or shed. Modern methods include bagging up dry apples in plastic bags, sealing the top, then piercing the plastic.

Quaking-grass (Briza) is a common meadow grass so you'll have no difficulty gathering enough to make a pretty wreath. Make a circle of wire for the base and build up the wreath by tying-in small bunches of the grass. It's easier to work with the stems quite long, and then trim them short when the wreath is finished. Other grasses to try include stiff, bristly coltsfoot (*Tussilago farfara*), Yorkshire fog (*Holcus lanatus*) and various bromes (Bromus).

When sweet chestnuts are ready to eat, the spiny case conveniently splits open. Take them home to roast in the fire for a celebratory autumn tea (remembering to nick the shells first or you'll have a series of explosions in the grate). Traditional iron shovels for holding chestnuts in the fire usually feature a pierced design to let the heat through.

Stored fruit should be checked regularly throughout winter for incipient rot. Any fruit showing the first signs of disease can be put out for the birds – blackbirds especially appreciate apples and pears. Add a dish of seeds and you have an instant bird-feeding station.

To give plum jam a sophisticated hint of almond, crack open the stones when you halve the plums and add the kernels along with the flesh. Or use the cracked stones to make *noyeau*, a French almond-flavoured liqueur: simply put them in a preserving jar, cover with vodka or eau de vie and leave in a cool, dark cupboard for at least three months.

Pumpkins and squashes are easy to grow. Sow the seed when all danger of frost is past in a well-manured plot. Once the plants have come through, keep them well watered. Protect prize specimens with a square of old carpet beneath, and harvest them before the first frost. Pumpkins and squashes can be stored throughout the winter if kept dry and frost-free.

Winter

*G*ETTING READY FOR CHRISTMAS

For many people all over the world, Christmas is now the most important celebration in the entire year. It's a very special occasion, and the culmination of weeks of preparation: baking and cooking, making decorations and homemade cards, choosing gifts and wrapping up presents.

Advent, the period that begins four Sundays before Christmas, is the traditional start to preparations. The Sunday before Advent, known as Stir Up Sunday, is a timely reminder to anyone who hasn't yet made their Christmas puddings or cake to get busy. In households where baking is done at home, the tradition still persists of each member of the family taking a turn at stirring the mixture – whether it be for fruitcake, mincemeat or Christmas puddings – and making a secret wish.

ABOVE: YOU DON'T HAVE TO PLUNDER THE BIRDS' WINTER LARDER TO MAKE A WREATH; ARTIFICIAL BERRIES LOOK JUST AS GOOD AS THE REAL THING.

FAR LEFT AND LEFT: A BARROW LOAD OF BLUE SPRUCE AND MISTLETOE TO DECORATE THE HOUSE. THE TWO EVERGREENS HAVE BEEN WIRED TOGETHER INTO A SIMPLE SPRAY NAILED OVER AN ANCIENT DOOR, WHICH ITSELF IS HUNG WITH A WREATH OF SNOWY GYPSOPHILA.

RIGHT: OUTDOOR TREE LIGHTS AND SMALL LANTERNS SET A GARDEN FENCE AGLOW WITH CHRISTMAS CHEER. IN THE UNITED STATES, HOUSE EXTERIORS HAVE FOR A LONG TIME BEEN AS LAVISHLY DECORATED AS THE INTERIORS – A WELCOMING CUSTOM THAT HAS CROSSED THE ATLANTIC.

On the first day of December, Advent calendars are often hung up containing stiff paper doors that children open, one by one, on each day leading up to Christmas. In modern versions, the wrapped chocolates tucked behind the doors are often more of an inducement than simple old-fashioned delight in whatever image lies behind.

Sometime during the ensuing weeks comes the moment that the whole family enjoys – fetching down the box of Christmas decorations from the top of the wardrobe or out of the attic. Intricately folded tissue paper bells and balls, snowmen and angels, skeins of tinsel and bags of artificial berries are all carefully lifted out and set in their rightful places. Then there are the decorations for the Christmas tree itself: shiny glass or metallic baubles, stitched and embroidered angels, a tangle of fairy lights, silver and gold stars, snowmen and Santas of every shape and size.

In some households a crib scene is displayed. This is a strong custom in France, especially in Provence, where the 'cast' of the Holy Family, shepherds, etc, is added to each year, with a new figure from the maker of the *santons*, or figurines. As well as familiar figures from the Christmas story, the *santons* often include characters from provincial life, such as a baker, onion seller or woman with a shopping basket.

Exchanging Christmas cards and decorating the house with paper chains, garlands and tinsel are relatively recent customs. In fact, many of the traditions we regard as part of a proper Christmas were the result of Victorian nostalgia for a time that never really existed. They were based on how Victorians imagined Christmas was celebrated in the early 17th century – when the festival was, in fact, a much more riotous affair (so much so that it was banned by the Puritan parliament and only restored, with the monarchy, 12 years later).

The Victorian author Charles Dickens gave Christmas celebrations a boost with the publication of *A Christmas Carol*, which described in detail all the elements of what we today regard as a traditional family Christmas. Some of the customs he wrote about were relatively unknown at the time, but middle-class families in both Britain and America soon adopted them.

Decorating the home with armfuls of greenery is a much older tradition, with a spiritual symbolism stretching back to pagan times. Once again, though, the Church was quick to take up the traditions for its own needs, and a home filled with greenery is now an essential part of Christmas.

ABOVE: CHRISTMAS BISCUITS WITH JEWELLED CENTRES ARE EASY TO MAKE. ROLL OUT THE BISCUIT DOUGH, STAMP OUT HEART SHAPES AND PLACE THEM ON A GREASED BAKING TRAY. BEFORE YOU PUT THEM IN THE OVEN, CUT OUT HEART-SHAPED CENTRES AND FILL THE GAP WITH CRUSHED BOILED SWEETS, WHICH WILL MELT AND FUSE WITH THE BISCUIT DOUGH. (TO MAKE THE HANGING HOLES, SEE PAGE 124.)

LEFT: A GARLAND OF FIR AND PINE CONES AND LAWSON CYPRESS FOR A MANTELPIECE. USE A LENGTH OF ROPE FOR THE BASE, AND WIRE THE CONES INDIVIDUALLY TO ATTACH THEM TO THE ROPE. ADD GREENERY TO HIDE THE WIRES. CANDLES ARE ALSO AN INDISPENSABLE PART OF CHRISTMAS DECORATIONS. BUT WHEREAS IN PAGAN TIMES THEY REPRESENTED THE HEAT AND LIGHT OF THE SUN IN THE DEAD OF WINTER, CHRISTIANS SEE THEM AS SYMBOLIZING THE LIGHT CHRIST SHEDS ON THE WORLD.

SEASONAL GREENERY AND WREATHS

Holly, ivy, mistletoe, fir, laurel, Lawson cypress and other evergreens are traditionally used to decorate the home at Christmas – sprigs are tucked behind pictures, clocks and mirrors, used to make swags for the mantelpiece or woven together in a Christmas wreath. In midwinter, when all other plants are dormant or dead, it's little wonder that evergreens came to be seen as tokens of continuity – proof that life goes on even in the bleakest season of the year.

Holly has long been regarded as a symbol of goodwill and friendship: the Romans used to exchange sprigs at the feast of Saturnalia in mid-December and decorate their houses with it for New Year. Superstitions abounded all over Europe concerning its magical, protective properties. As Christianity spread, holly was neatly absorbed into Christian symbolism, its prickles representing Christ's crown of thorns and the red berries his blood.

Ivy may be a relic of more drunken Christmas celebrations. The Romans associated it with their god of wine, Bacchus. Many years later, it was trained to grow up a pole outside taverns to indicate wine and ale on sale.

According to one legend, mistletoe was originally a tree, and its timber was used to build the cross on which Christ was crucified, after which it dwindled to a feeble parasitic plant in shame. In fact, mistletoe had played a big role in the religious rites of the Druids, who believed it had miraculous healing properties and was a sign of fertility, and they hung it in their places of worship. The plant has always been shunned by the Church, perhaps because of its role in these ancient magic and fertility rites. Nevertheless, the practice of hanging up mistletoe in the home has persisted right up to the present day, and the custom of kissing under it may possibly derive from the Druidic fertility rites.

Mistletoe was a major element in the 'kissing bough', which in medieval times was often the centrepiece of Christmas decorations in the home. The kissing bough underwent something of a revival in the early 20th century, when it was seen to be more truly British than the imported Christmas tree. It was far more complicated to make than

RIGHT: A HOMEMADE WREATH OF BAY LEAVES AND CRAB APPLES TUCKED INTO A WOVEN BASE SHOULD OUTLAST THE FESTIVITIES. ANTIQUE CHRISTMAS CARDS MAKE MORE ENDURING DECORATIONS AND ARE HIGHLY COLLECTABLE.

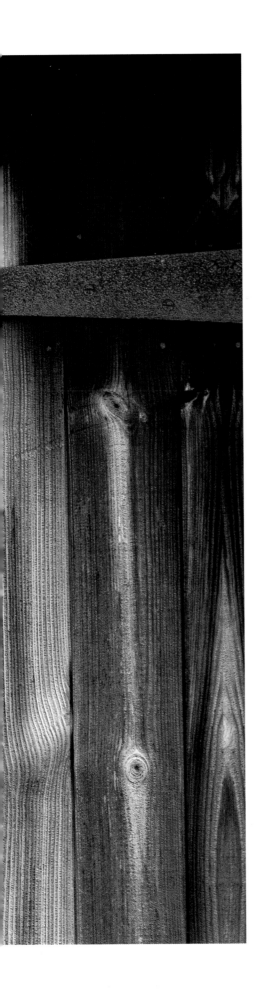

any wreath, as this contemporary account shows: 'Five equal circles of thickish, not too pliable wire, say 1ft 9ins in diameter, are bound together so that one becomes the horizontal "equator", with the four others crossing at the "poles", to form eight meridians.' It was bound with tape and covered with box clippings; seven red apples were suspended at the centre of the globe, 'hung on red ribbons, taken right through the core with a bodkin and knotted below'. Eight red candles were fixed around the 'equator', and another eight at each 'meridian' lower down. A great bunch of mistletoe was tied below and finally, the device was hung up, 'on red cords perhaps'.

However elaborate or simple the greenery, tradition dictates that Christmas decorations should be removed after Epiphany, or Twelfth Night. Whether this means January 5th or January 6th – that is, the eve of the Twelfth Day or the night of Twelfth Day – itself is still hotly disputed. In a few places, Christmas greenery was not taken down until Candlemas, on February 2nd, when snowdrops were picked to replace it (see page 13).

Whatever we believe about their symbolism, evergreens can still be appreciated for their form and beauty and used to make the home look festive. Although market stalls and florists sell readymade sprays and wreaths, they are easy and satisfying to make yourself, and you can embellish them with extra materials from garden and hedgerow.

To make a wreath you need to start with a base. Holly, ivy, mistletoe and other evergreens will last for ten days or so without browning and withering if simply wired onto a wicker or vine wreath base. However, if you are using less robust greenery or fresh flowers, you'll need a wreath base that retains moisture. Florists sell moss bases that can be pre-soaked before being decorated then dampened every two or three days, and also circular trays that hold florist's-foam rings, which have a much larger water-holding capacity. For wicker or vine wreaths, use florist's wires to attach materials, but for moss or florist's-foam bases you can simply push flowers and leaves firmly into them. Make sure you hang up the wreath securely, because a wet wreath packed with greenery can be heavy.

LEFT: SPRIGS OF SPRUCE AND EUCALYPTUS SCENT A WREATH COMPOSED OF BOTH DRIED AND FRESH INGREDIENTS. TRADITIONAL IVY AND PINE CONES ARE SUPPLEMENTED BY LOTUS SEEDHEADS, NUTS, CINNAMON-STICK BUNDLES AND SMALL DRIED ARTICHOKE FLOWERS.

CHRISTMAS TREES

Bringing a tree indoors at Christmas was originally a German custom and dates back to medieval times. As German emigrants established communities around the world, so the practice spread. One of the first German settlements in the United States was in Pennsylvania, where they continued the tradition of decorating a tree at Christmas, using whatever was available. Thus, in the New World, trees were hung with cranberries, apples, nuts, marzipan cookies and garlands of dyed popcorn.

In Britain, Christmas trees didn't become popular until the 1840s, when Prince Albert's passion for spectacularly decorated trees inspired his subjects to follow suit. This is how the Royal tree of Christmas 1848 was described in the *Illustrated London News*: 'The tree... is a young fir of about eight feet [2.5 metres] high, and has six tiers of branches. On each tier or branch are arranged a dozen wax tapers. Pendant from the branches are elegant trays, baskets, bonbonnières, and other receptacles for sweetmeats of the most varied and expensive kind... Fancy cakes, gilt gingerbreads and eggs filled with sweetmeats are also suspended by variously coloured ribbons from the branches.'

For many years, the Norway spruce was the only tree commonly sold at Christmas, but today the choice has improved. Lodgepole pines are popular for their distinctive brown buds, the Fraser fir and noble fir are prized for their bluish needles, while the grand fir smells sweetest of all. Displaying the decorated Christmas tree in the window so that it can be seen from the street is a relatively recent – and very welcome – custom.

BELOW LEFT: INSTEAD OF THE USUAL FIR, A VARIEGATED STANDARD HOLLY TREE IS BROUGHT IN FROM THE GARDEN AND HUNG WITH HOMEMADE BISCUITS IN THE SHAPE OF BELLS, STARS AND DOVES. THIS IS A TREE THAT CAN BE USED YEAR AFTER YEAR.

BELOW: TRANSFORM ORDINARY FAIRY LIGHTS BY MAKING TINY SHADES FROM CRAFT FOIL. CUT OUT THE SHADES USING A CRAFT KNIFE, THEN FOLD AND GLUE THEM INTO SHAPE. MAKE A HANDLE FOR EACH SHADE TO LOOP OVER THE FAIRY-LIGHT WIRE AND HOLD IT IN PLACE.

BELOW, LEFT AND CENTRE: SAVE SMALL SCRAPS
OF FABRIC TO MAKE RUSTIC CHRISTMAS TREE
DECORATIONS SUCH AS THIS SIMPLE MINIATURE
RAG DOLL AND CALICO TEDDY – OR LOOK OUT
FOR SIMILAR HANDMADE DECORATIONS AT
CHRISTMAS CRAFT FAIRS.

RIGHT: GILDED WALNUTS, FABRIC HEARTS, APPLES
AND GINGERBREAD BISCUITS DECORATE A TREE
TOPPED BY A STAR OF SPRAYED GOLD LEAVES AND
BRACKEN. REAL CANDLES ILLUMINATE THE TREE –
ALWAYS EXTINGUISH THEM WHEN YOU LEAVE
THE ROOM.

GIFTS AND GIFT WRAPPING

Giving presents at Christmas carries on the tradition begun by the Three Wise Men when they brought gifts to the Holy Child. There is, however, an even earlier precedent for this custom, as the ancient Romans used to exchange gifts at New Year. Nevertheless, gift-giving did not become a Christian tradition until the Middle Ages, and the custom of wrapping gifts only appeared in the mid-19th century. The wrapping paper then was generally brown and was embellished by hand with fancy cut-out scraps of paper, frills and spangles.

Plain brown parcel paper can be used today as a basis for imaginative gift wraps as it is tough enough to take elaborate paint designs and makes a surprisingly sophisticated background for them. Unusual wrapping can make a present stand out from the rest and turn it into the most intriguing of all the packages under the Christmas tree. If you don't feel confident about wielding a brush, consider stamping. It's quick, easy and effective, and at this time of year stationers' shops stock rubber stamps embossed with seasonal shapes – stars, angels, doves, etc. Or you could make your own stamps from potato halves: the conventional method is to cut around your chosen motif so that it stands proud from the potato surface, but it is also possible to cut away within the motif so that the potato background takes up the paint instead. In addition, customize plain luggage tags or ordinary sticky labels, continuing the theme.

Awkwardly shaped presents are harder to wrap. Turning them into a cracker shape using masses of coloured tissue paper is one solution. Tie both ends with ribbon or string and add a fresh flower or Christmas greenery just before you hand the present over.

ABOVE LEFT: PLAIN BROWN PAPER CAN BE CUSTOMIZED USING STAMPS AND SILVER PAINT. PERSONALIZE BOUGHT GIFT BOXES WITH RUSTIC STRING AND A DECORATIVE CINNAMON STICK.

LEFT: AN OLD TIN JELLY MOULD MAKES A PERFECT CONTAINER FOR HOMEMADE SWEETS.

RIGHT: THE GIVEAWAY SHAPE OF BOTTLES CAN BE CONCEALED WITH LAYERS OF TISSUE PAPER. YOU CAN'T DISGUISE A PLANT LIKE THIS AMARYLLIS SO MAKE A FEATURE OF IT INSTEAD.

THE CHRISTMAS TABLE

The highlight of the Christmas festival is a splendid dinner. Feasting has long been associated with Christmas, and in pagan times, with midwinter festivals. However, the traditional Christmas dinner we enjoy today dates from the mid-19th century, when many of the old customs were revived and some new ones introduced. It was at this time that turkey became popular, even though it had been brought back from the New World three centuries earlier. Before that, goose was the traditional Christmas fare, while in grand establishments roast peacock was the order of the day. The traditional finish to the meal, plum pudding served flaming with brandy, had its origins in a Celtic porridge known as frumenty, which developed into the medieval plum pottage and eventually into plum pudding.

Whether or not you are serving a full traditional dinner, the table has an important role to play in showing the food to its best advantage. Glittering crystal, china and silver, crisp linen and golden candlelight all enhance the atmosphere and set the scene.

PREVIOUS PAGES: THE TRADITIONAL LIGHTING OF CANDLES ON A WINDOWSILL AT TWILIGHT.

LEFT: A FESTIVE TABLE DRESSED FOR DINNER IN RED AND WHITE.

BELOW LEFT: A VINTAGE CRACKER FOR A TRADITIONAL PLACE SETTING. CRACKERS WERE DEVISED IN THE 19TH CENTURY BY ENGLISHMAN TOM SMITH.

BELOW: ENAMELLED WINEGLASSES ARE THE ULTIMATE IN OPULENCE. WHETHER ANTIQUE OR MODERN, THEY WILL BE TREASURED EACH CHRISTMAS.

CAROL SINGING

Carols have been sung at Christmas since medieval times. Like other forms of folk song, they were rarely written down – instead, they survived by being passed from generation to generation. Nineteenth-century antiquarians, worried by the unreliability of oral tradition and folk memory, took to the road and travelled the length and breadth of the country, writing down the words and music of ancient carols so that they should not be lost. Following the publication of their findings, some of the more obscure carols reached a wider audience, typically through ballad sellers who stood on city street corners and sold printed song sheets. Some of the finest carols were written during the 18th century, when religious reformers used them as a way of promoting Christianity. 'Hark the Herald Angels Sing', for example, was written by Charles Wesley, the Methodist evangelist. Carols from other countries, such as the German 'Silent Night', were translated into English at this time, too.

BELOW LEFT: IN DAYS GONE BY, CHOIRS OF CAROL SINGERS WOULD SERENADE THE WHOLE VILLAGE, CALLING FINALLY AT THE MANOR HOUSE, WHERE THEY HOPED TO BE PLIED WITH MINCE PIES AND HOT PUNCH. THESE DAYS, PEOPLE ARE MORE LIKELY TO ATTEND A SPECIAL CAROL SERVICE IN THE CHURCH.

BELOW: PRINTED SONG SHEETS AVOID DISHARMONY IN THE RANKS.

RIGHT: CANDLELIT LANTERNS ADD TO THE FESTIVE AIR AND CAN BE EITHER HAND-HELD OR HUNG FROM A STURDY BRANCH.

NEW YEAR'S EVE

Since time immemorial, people have gathered together to welcome the coming year and to wish each other well. In Scotland, New Year has traditionally been a more important celebration than Christmas. In the Scottish custom known as 'first-footing', a loud knocking at the door as the last stroke of midnight dies away heralds the arrival of a dark-haired stranger bearing mistletoe, bread, salt and coal. The stranger represents the New Year itself, arriving uninvited, and he cannot be turned away. The bread, salt and coal are symbols of hospitality. As for the mistletoe, he usually takes it around the room to kiss all the women.

If you are planning a dinner party for New Year's Eve, a sophisticated white and silver table setting makes a cool contrast to an opulent Christmas table yet still looks suitably festive. Leave plenty of time for fun and games after dinner – and try to arrange for a dark-haired stranger to call at midnight.

THIS PAGE AND RIGHT: SET AN ELEGANT WHITE TABLE FOR A NEW YEAR'S EVE DINNER. PLAIN WHITE EVERYDAY CHINA IS ENRICHED WITH SUBTLE TOUCHES OF GOLD ON GLASSWARE, AND GILDED GRAPES, PINE CONES AND LEAVES. CONTINUE THE THEME BY HANGING DELICATE PAPER SNOWFLAKES AT THE WINDOW, EMBELLISHING NUTS AND HOLLY LEAVES WITH A COAT OF SILVER SPRAY PAINT (STIPPLED WITH BLACK FOR AUTHENTIC ANTIQUITY) AND LIGHTING WHITE LANTERNS.

RINGING IN THE NEW YEAR

As midnight approaches on New Year's Eve and festivities reach a crescendo, bell-ringers gather in churches all over the land to welcome the New Year. Where there is just one bell, midnight is tolled on a single joyful note, but where the church boasts a full set, a cheerful peal of bells greets the New Year. In Britain the bells are rung not in unison but one after another, with the sequence changing after each round.

In many villages this is the signal for people to spill out of pubs and parties to stand and listen, then wish each other a Happy New Year. Once it also gave an ardent suitor the chance to rush to his sweetheart's door and wait there to be the first to greet her in the New Year. Some families still like to leave the house just before midnight, and when they return, let the youngest member cross the threshold first before the whole household follows suit.

When Queen Victoria was on the throne, she decided one year that New Year at the Palace should be heralded with a triumphant blast of trumpets. She later noted, 'This had a fine solemn effect which quite affected dear Albert, who turned pale, and had tears in his eyes, and pressed my hand very warmly.'

THIS PAGE AND RIGHT: CHURCH BELLS ARE AN INTEGRAL PART OF VILLAGE LIFE AND ARE RUNG TO USHER IN THE NEW YEAR. BELLS ARE TUNED TO MUSICAL NOTES – FROM TENOR TO TREBLE. SOME BELL TOWERS HAVE AS MANY AS 12 BELLS. WHEN THE BELL-RINGER PULLS A ROPE, IT TURNS A WHEEL MECHANISM WHICH CAUSES THE BELL TO RING AS IT SWINGS IN A FULL CIRCLE. IN SOME EUROPEAN AND AMERICAN CITY CHURCHES, UP TO 74 BELLS ARE HOUSED IN A SPECIAL TOWER; THESE *CARILLONS* ARE PLAYED FROM A KEYBOARD.

Gilding leaves, dried or evergreen, is an effective and inexpensive traditional way to make Christmas decorations. Laurel and bay, both evergreen, lend themselves particularly well to this treatment as they have broad, shiny leaves. Gold spray paint, available from artists' suppliers, is the easiest way to gild the leaves, but always use it in a well-ventilated room, or work outside on a still day. Protect your immediate surroundings with newspaper. Silver paint is equally effective, depending on your colour scheme.

Spicy pomanders, made from oranges studded with cloves, have an unmistakably Christmassy perfume. They are quite satisfying to make, and pricking rows of holes in the peel with a bodkin or darning needle makes it easier to push in the cloves. (Don't pack them too close together, because the orange shrinks a little as it dries.) When the fruit is covered, leave it to dry in a warm place for three to four weeks, then add a ribbon loop. Orange slices or whole fruits can be dried in a very cool oven until hard, then finished off in the same way. The same methods work for other citrus fruits.

Create your own Christmas wreath to hang on the front door. Either buy a ready-made base (available from florists) or make your own from a circlet of wire padded with clumps of moss. The moss can be wired to the circlet with short lengths of florists' wire. Once the base is established, decorate with whatever takes your fancy – pine cones, fruit, berries, foliage, fabric, braid or candles. Don't be tempted to light the candles as they will be surrounded by flammable

Make your own Christmas gift bags from plain paper carriers. Cut images from last year's Christmas cards and use photo corners to attach them to the front of the carrier, or simply glue them in place. Add a gingham bow – wired ribbon is best for tying a firm, free-standing bow – and wrap the gift in swathes of crumpled coloured tissue paper to conceal it within the bag.

Embellish plain white candles with pressed leaves: here, ferns and ginkgo leaves have been used. Melt some paraffin wax, available from candle-maker's suppliers, in a double boiler and dip the leaves into the melted wax. Press them quickly onto the candle, then dip the entire candle into the melted wax to give an even finish. Keep an eye on the lit candle when the flame reaches the level of the leaf decorations, just in case they ignite.

Homemade beeswax candles take just minutes to make. Buy sheets of beeswax and a roll of appropriate wick from a candle-maker's suppliers – wicks are sold to match the finished diameter of the candle. For best results, work in a warm room or gently warm the beeswax sheets with a hairdryer before you start. Then place a length of wick at the edge of a sheet and simply roll the sheet up tightly. Press the final edge firmly against the candle to prevent it from unrolling. Trim the wick to 1cm (½in) before lighting.

Use garden herbs to scent a Christmas wreath. Sprigs of rosemary and cotton lavender (Santolina) give this simple wreath its fresh fragrance, supplemented by stems of dried lavender woven into the base. Tiny alder cones have been used along with the more familiar pine cones. Chinese lanterns (Physalis) and rowan berries (*Sorbus aucuparia*) add a burst of colour – the latter are reputed to keep witches away.

Homemade dried-fruit loaves of various kinds are traditional Christmas fare all over Europe and America – *panforte* from Italy and *birewecke* from Alsace can include raisins, cherries, pears and figs; *stollen*, from Germany, is enriched with almond paste. Choose your favourite recipe and bake a batch to give as gifts. For simplicity, wrap loaves in plain greaseproof paper secured with a ribbon. Because the recipes use little or no fat, the loaves store well.

If you can't bear to throw away the prettiest Christmas cards, gift tags and scraps of ribbon each year, then turn them into a lasting memento by pasting them into a scrapbook or Christmas album. You'll be carrying on a tradition from the Victorian era, when Christmas cards, having just been invented, were far too precious to be discarded. Add to your album every year and you'll build up a pictorial history of your Christmases past, especially if you add handwritten recipes or magazine cuttings, details of menus – and a good selection of photos.

When you're decorating the house at Christmas, don't forget the windows. They give visitors a hint of what's to come inside and create a welcoming display. Cut-paper snowflakes can be hung at the window without fear of obscuring too much precious daylight, and iced Christmas biscuits can be hung from the window catch. Ensure they are robust enough by using a gingerbread or shortbread mix. To make a hole for a ribbon loop, use a drinking straw to pierce the biscuits just after removing them from the oven, before they have had time to harden.

Shiny red apples contrast with papery dried red hydrangea heads in this indoor wreath. As apples are heavy, they need to be securely wired onto a stout moss wreath. Use a florist's stub wire and pierce the apple right through the lower third of the fruit, then pass the ends of the wire through the wreath base and twist them together. Make sure the wreath is hung from a strong hook or masonry nail.

Beautifully wrapped presents make a memorable impression – and ingenuity counts for more than expensive papers. Flat parcels, such as books or boxes, can be plainly wrapped in old-fashioned sugar paper or recycled paper then trimmed with ribbon. Start with a wide ribbon, then add a narrower one in either a contrasting or a toning colour and finish with a length of ricrac. Glue or sew the ends of the ricrac together, then glue or sew on a small bow to cover the join.

Use the layering technique described below left to dress up jars of homemade biscuits, sweets or preserves for gifts. Because ribbon would be too slippery on glass jars, use layers of paper to create a similar effect. Make a decorative edge to the bands of paper using pinking shears and scalloped scissors, and secure them in place with a narrow ribbon. A few blobs of glue may be needed to help hold everything neatly together.

Don't discard scraps and trimmings from wreath and garland making: put them to good use elsewhere. With a bit of bending and coaxing, the end of a blue-spruce branch will form a readymade five-pointed star. Adding a gift tag inscribed with the guest's name turns it into an imaginative place setting.

Thoughtful packaging lifts any present out of the ordinary. Here a batch of homemade meringues has been wrapped in a haze of clear cellophane and tied, cracker-style, at each end with a length of gauzy ribbon. It's a simple idea that can be used to enclose sweets, biscuits or even slices of Christmas cake for guests to take home with them.

To make an eye-catching table centrepiece, half fill a shallow bowl with water and add a flotilla of floating candles. If you have a few roses or camellia heads to spare, float these in the bowl for an even more glamorous effect. The most traditional flower to use would be the Christmas rose (*Helleborus niger*), whose pure white flowers were once cultivated specially for sale at Christmas. Floating candles are widely available and come in all shapes and sizes, but avoid scented versions, which may be too powerfully perfumed for the dinner table.

INDEX

Bold page numbers refer to
'Practicalities'; *italic* numbers
refer to photographs.

PHOTOGRAPHIC ACKNOWLEDGMENTS

Caroline Arber 8, 31 (top), 32 (second from bottom), 33 (bottom), 44, 45, 46 (left and right), 54-55, 56 (left), 57 (right), 58 (left and right), 59 (left), 68 (second from bottom), 69 (top, second and third from top), 70 (top), 120, 121
Graham Atkins-Hughes 87 (left and top right)
Jan Baldwin 52 (left), 53
Nick Brown 62 (left), 67
Charlie Colmer 10-11, 12, 12-13, 13, 16 (left and right), 17, 18, 32 (second from top), 33 (top), 50, 75, 76 (top), 77, 94 (second from top), 96 (second from top), 108 (left), 112-113
Harry Cory-Wright 7, 39 (top and bottom), 72-73, , 74 (top and bottom), 78-79, 80-81, 86, 97 (top and third from top), 106, 122 (second from top), 123 (second and third from top)
Christopher Drake 15 (left), 47 (right), 96 (third from top)
Tim Evan-Cook 52 (right)
Laurie Evans 48, 49 (top and bottom), 56 (right), 57 (left), 68 (top)
Craig Fordham 59 (right), 116, 117 (left and right)
Kate Gadsby 87 (bottom right), 89, 97 (bottom)
David George 109 (right), 124 (second and third from top), 125 (second from top)
Huntley Hedworth 32 (bottom)
Graham Kirk 36, 42 (top and bottom), 43

Peter Knab 30 (top)
James Merrell 123 (top), 125 (bottom)
Debbie Patterson 71 (second from top)
Nick Pope 40-41, 68 (second from top), 68 (second from top and bottom), 70 (bottom), 71 (top and third from top)
Trevor Richards 123 (bottom), 125 (third from top)
Kim Sayer 119
Heini Schneebeli 88 (top and bottom), 91, 96 (top)
Ron Sutherland 60 (left and right), 61, 62 (right), 63, 64-65, 66, 69 (bottom), 70 (second from top)
Debi Treloar 24, 31 (second and third from top), 105, 124 (top)
Pia Tryde 1, 3, 14, 15 (right), 20-21, 22, 23 (left and right), 25, 26, 27, 28 (left and right), 29, 30 (bottom), 31 (bottom), 32 (top), 33 (second and third from top), 34-35, 38, 47 (left), 70 (second from bottom), 76 (bottom), 82 (top and bottom), 83, 84, 85 (left and right), 92-93, 94 (top, third from top and bottom), 95, 97 (second from top), 98-99, 100, 101, 102, 103, 108 (right), 109 (left and centre), 110 (top and bottom), 111, 114, 115 (left and right), 118, 122 (top and bottom), 124 (bottom), 125 (top)
Tim Winter 37

Styling by Hester Page, Ben Kendrick, Pippa Rimmer, Gabi Tubbs and Margaret Caselton.